Effective Presentation

(How to Create and Deliver a Winning Presentation)

Published by :
Lotus Press Publishers & Distributors

Effective Presentation

(How to Create and Deliver a Winning Presentation)

Kiran Kaushik

4735/22, Prakash Deep Building
Ansari Road, Darya Ganj,
New Delhi - 110002

Lotus Press : Publishers & Distributors
Unit No. 220, 2nd Floor, 4735/22, Prakash Deep Building,
Ansari Road, Darya Ganj, New Delhi- 110002
Ph.: 23280047, 98118-38000
• E-mail : lotuspress1984@gmail.com
www.lotuspress.co.in

Effective Presentation

ISBN: 81-8382-167-7

Printed & Published by : **Lotus Press Publishers & Distributors,** New Delhi-02

PREFACE

The truly diligent and savvy corporate executive of today can heartily recognise and acknowledge the need for effective presentation of projects. The corporate world does not only deal with inter-enterprise competition, but also intra-enterprise confrontations, which creates competition amongst corporate employees.

In such a scenario of intense pressure, there is hardly space for complacency or a backadisical attitude; contemporary work ethics call for spright and confidence in every step of corporate work. One such facet of corporate work is project presentation, which, although being the mode of final, theoretical work representation, is really the beginning of corporate reality. As such, the crucial nature of presentations cannot be ignored, and an effective one, which charms all those who are witness to it, is most undoutably and obviously a valuable asset to a corporate employee.

This book, conceptualised and written as a corporate work manual, concentrates on the arena of project presentation. It engages the readers in an comprehensive, incisive discussion of the principles of great presentation, especially in relation to marketing, advertising or project initiation. In addition, it bring to attention, issues of evolving market, etc., and how they all are necessarily to be kept in mind while making a presentation.

Editor

CONTENTS

1

HOW TO MAKE AN EFFECTIVE PRESENTATION

A great presentation is a combination of the three elements: content, design, and delivery. Content includes the research and organisation of materials. Design is the architecture of the slides and the graphical enhancements. Delivery is how you voice your message. To make the presentation great, there must be synergy of these three elements. Each of these elements carries equal weight and importance. Your presentation will not be great unless you have all three of these elements.

For example, let's say you don't do a good job researching and organising your content, but you spend hours designing the presentation with all the bells and whistles and hours practicing your delivery. What's going to happen when you get in front of your audience? You're going to run through your presentation and it won't be interactive because you don't know more than what's on your slides. Your audience is going to pay attention to the next sound or wild animation.

When someone asks you questions, you're not going to know the answers, which will severely hurt your credibility. The audience will take little or nothing back from the content of your presentation and you will look unprofessional as a presenter. By properly combining content, design, and delivery, you'll create a great presentation!

ELEMENTS OF EFFECTIVE PRESENTATION

Process

There is a process to creating that great presentation. First, you must create your content. Then, you must design for that content. Finally, you must develop your delivery strategy and style.

Content

There are some key steps to keep in mind when creating your content. First, you do your research. Then, group the information into logical categories. Finally, you create your outline.

Too often presenters don't follow those key steps. The night before a meeting, they're cramming information onto slides trying to create this great presentation. They may even be adding items to their presentation at the last minute.

To avoid the problems of late preparation and last-minute editing, think of creating the content of your presentation in terms of these three steps:

1. Do your research.
2. Group your information into logical categories.
3. Create your outline.

Design

Once you've outlined your presentation, you're ready to create your slides and add graphics, charts, and animation. .

Delivery

And finally, there's the delivery. You need to know the logistics of your meeting. You need to understand how to make the participants retain your message. You need to set clear objectives in the presentation as well as state your expectations for your audience. They need to find value in your presentation. Your presentation needs to be such that what you present and how you present it causes a change in behavior of those who attend the presentation. Maybe it's a case of helping them to better understand the long-range vision of the company; if you can get them to see i in a way that helps them embrace change, improves morale, and increases productivity, your presentation has done the job.

The Situation

When you decide or find out that you're going to do a presentation, get all of the details. This advice might seem obvious, but some people immediately start thinking and/or worrying about what they'll do, getting at least one big step ahead of themselves before they really know where they're going. The details that you should get will generally fall into four categories, which you can remember as the four P's:

— Purpose

— People

— Point

— Place

Purpose

Why are you doing this presentation? The full answer to that question is your purpose. And that full answer has two parts. The first part is your subject area, the *what* of your presentation. What will you be addressing or covering? The proposed changes in the employee manual? The recent negative media reports about the new product? The update of the company intranet?

It's essential to find out how broad or narrow your scope should be and how deep you should go—aspects that depend to a great extent on the other P's. It may be just as important to find out if there's anything that you should avoid, such as a proposal that the board is still debating or a recent resignation in the department that developed the new product.

The second part of your purpose is the reason, the *why* of your presentation. What are you expected to do? Provide information? Help participants understand? Persuade them to agree on something? Motivate them to act? Entertain them? There may be several reasons for doing the presentation. Unless you know them all, it's not likely that you'll balance and structure your presentation appropriately.

The full answer to the *why* question may not come easily—or at all. Sometimes you have to ask and then ask again—and sometimes you have to figure out the rest of the answer by yourself.

The *why* of your purpose is probably as important as the *what*—and it often may be even more important. If it makes sense to ask, do so. If it's wiser to find out on your own, do so. You don't want to find out about hidden agendas or unexpressed expectations too late.

People

To whom are you delivering this presentation? The answer to that question may seem simple enough, especially if you know the target group. But make sure you know how much or how little they know about the subject of your presentation and why they need to know any more.

You might imagine yourself sitting among those people.

Answer the following key questions:

— Why are you attending this presentation?

— How do you feel about attending it?

— What do you expect to get out of it?

If you can't imagine how those people would answer those questions, maybe you don't have a good enough sense of who they are. Find out more about them until you can answer those questions with confidence.

Point

What do you want to happen as a result of your presentation? That's the point, the objective.

How will the participants be different because of your presentation? In other words, what will be evidence that you succeeded, that you met your expectations?

If you know your purpose, why you're doing the presentation, you should have little trouble figuring out the point. (Now, as for reaching the point, well, that's where things get more complicated. . . .)

Place

Where are you doing the presentation? And don't settle for just a room designation—unless you know all about that location. Here some questions to answer:

— How big is the room?

— What is the layout of seats and other furniture? How much can it be changed, if needed?

— Where are you going to be in that room?

— What equipment will be in that room? A screen? A microphone? (What kind?) A podium?

— Where are the electrical outlets?

— Where is the connection for the intranet and/or Internet?

— How good is the lighting and how is it controlled?

— How well does the heating and air conditioning work?

— Are there windows? If so, how many, how big, and where are they? Is the view likely to distract participants? Are there curtains?

— Is the room relatively quiet? How likely is it that there will be disruptions?

You may not need to ask all of these questions, depending on the nature of your presentation. You may already have most or all of the answers. But it's always smartest to make sure. Finally, a question that's related to location only in that it's also a logistics issue: How much time will you have for your presentation?

PRESENTATION CHECKLISTS

Every time you create a presentation, you use these checklists as guidelines for helping you to make that presentation be as effective and successful as you hope it will be.

Total Visual Checklist

The first checklist is the Total Visual Checklist. Use this one for the entire presentation. It helps you with the organisation, the content, and the look of the presentation. Use this when you're reviewing your presentation as a whole.

Attribute	*Description*
Organisation	
Agenda	Present the agenda within the first three slides.
Logical Flow	Ensure that the flow follows the agenda and is easy for the audience to follow.
Data Clustering	Check that all information related to one topic is together.
Account	
Customisation	Include placeholders for account information.
Blank or Logo Screen	Include blank or logo slides as the first and last slides of the presentation.
Appendix	Include an appendix for easy reference for the audience.
Hidden Slides	Use hidden slides that contain additional details; use only if needed.
Content/Flow	
Variety	Vary the slides. For example, don't show six pie charts or six bullet slides in a row. Change slide style approximately every 3-5 slides.
Appropriate Chart	Ensure that the type of chart you choose is the best way to display the data.
Transitions	Build transitional phrases into your speaking notes.
Necessity of Slide	Cut out unnecessary slides. Create hidden slides or hyperlinks to address questions that might be asked.
Look	
Appropriate Template	Ensure that the template matches presentation objective, presentation medium, and content. Determine how best to use sidebars, titles, and footers. Determine background colour: light or dark. Use best contrast: light text on dark background.
Informative Headings	Use different headings that provide instant identification of the main point/content of slide.

(Contd....)

(Contd....)

Presentation Medium	Use colour, black and white, or textures in charts and graphs, based on the presentation method. For example, don't use yellow text if black and white hard copies will be left behind; yellow text can't be seen on white paper.
Graphics	Ensure that the graphics accurately and appropriately represent the topic and message. Use appropriate graphics for your message: for a reference to something, use a symbol or clip art; for an accurate representation, use a picture or video.

Single Visual Checklist

For each individual slide, use the Single Visual Checklist. This will help you review the organisation, understanding, look, and flow for each individual slide.

Attribute	*Description*
Organisation	
Major Point	Have only one major point on each slide.
Focal Point	Create one primary point of focus on each slide.
Concise	Leave out information the presenter can say.
Understanding	
Titles	Write informative titles that tell your audience the importance of the slide within three seconds.
Illustrate	Illustrate information with charts, comparison tables, and/or pictures.
Call Attention	Use arrows or symbols that draw attention to the important part of the chart or diagram.
Interpretation	Build into your speaker's notes an explanation of why the data is important.
Charts	Keep the charts simple, with a clear focus. Make sure that data points are well placed and easy to read.
Abbreviations	Use abbreviations only when the audience will understand.
Phrases	Use phrases; not sentences.

(Contd....)

(Contd....)

Parallel Structure	Ensure that all phrases start the same way, with all ve bs or all nouns.
Limited Words	Add the fewest words needed to explain a picture or chart. Put full explanation in your speaker's notes to enable presenter to discuss.
Fonts	Use 24-point font for text; no less than 20, if absolutely necessary. Use a sans serif type face, such as Tahoma or Arial.
Clip Art	Use only to enhance a point; avoid cartoon clip art in most cases.
Sizing Photos/ Clip Art	Ensure that images are sized to the appropriate scale.
Spell Check	Check spelling of bullet points and chart information. Use software tool and check visually.
Flow	
Photographs	Ensure that there's enough memory to have photos come up quickly. Use JPEG format at a low resolution (72dpi).
Builds	Use builds to emphasize and speak on one bullet point at a time. Choose transitions that are simple and easy on the eyes.

EFFECTIVE VISUAL PRESENTATION

The central purpose of any presentation, written, oral or visual, is communication. To communicate effectively, you must state your facts in a simple, concise and interesting manner. It is proven that the people learn more readily and retain more information when learning is reinforced by visualisation. You can entertain, inform, excite and even shock an audience by the proper integration of visual images into virtually any exchange of information.

Meetings which might normally be considered dull, or a chore to be avoided, can be transformed into exciting productions that grab the attention of the viewers. This kind of presentation maximises the audience retention of the subject matter. The phrase *"a picture is worth a thousand words"* has existed since the New York Post discovered the value of visuals in the news business. This remains true to this day. Simple, clear, concise visual images, briskly paced and sprinkled with attention-grabbing graphics will lend support to your spoken words. This leaves your audience with a positive attitude toward you and your product, service or proposal.

Visuals in business should be used in support of the spoken or written word, and not in lieu of it. A well-developed concept and effective script are the essential elements of any presentation. Regardless of their form, they should be the first and most important phase of its development. When the concept begins to take final form, the visuals are developed around it.

This is not to imply that A-V design should be placed near the end of the project. You must begin mentally planning your visuals at the beginning of the design process. Hastily designed and produced visuals can doom a presentation (and a presenter,) where well planned and executed images add tremendous strength. Concepts that are difficult to grasp can be communicated quickly and easily through the intelligent use of professionally produced visuals. This allows you the freedom to communicate more complex subject matter in a more efficient manner, adding support and impact to your script.

Finally, your presentation should be entertaining. Leave the audience feeling better and more relaxed when they leave and that impression will carry over to both your subject matter and yourself. There is no logical reason that the presentation of routine sales figures and financial reports should not be as exciting as the unveiling of a new product or a first rate service proposal.

Steps to Effective Visual Presentation

1. *Know your subject matter*

While this first point may seem obvious, it is very important that you research every nuance of your subject. Read reports and look up information about the subject with the specific purpose of writing a presentation script. When examined in this light, new ideas and alternative ways of thinking often develop. The ability to present a subject with confidence directly affects your audience's impressions and will help keep their attention.

This is especially important when giving a design presentation or proposal since you are in effect selling" your ideas to the audience. This applies whether the audience is a potential client or your own board of directors.

2. *Know your audience*

A small amount of research into the makeup of your audience will reap large benefits on presentation day.

If you were travelling about speaking on behalf of a new construction project you would tailor vastly different presentations to an audience of engineers and other concerning agencies. You'd should also have a couple of other versions for local community activist groups.

Before you 're-purpose' your *Teamsters* speech for use make the obvious adjustments and then carefully review your content from the 'philosophical' viewpoint of your audience.

If a small amount of research will help you, imagine what a moderate amount will do!

3. *Know yourself*

We all must push our limits and willingly bite off more

than we may be comfortable swallowing on occasion — this is how we learn and grow. Knowing a few of your limits, however, might avert disaster, or at least embarassment.

Intimately related to *Know Your Audience* above, your 'limits' are just where you may or may not tread, depending on the makeup of your audience and your relationship with them.

4. Develop a theme

All presentations, regardless of their complexity, are designed with a single purpose. Whether that purpose is to sell, educate, or for pure entertainment, state that purpose to yourself at the beginning of the development process. Always keep this purpose in mind.

5. Prepare your script

The script does not necessarily have to be a work of literary excellence. For some, simple notes on 3 x 5 file cards are sufficient. Other presenters and presentations require a carefully composed, professionally developed script. The exact form of the script depends on the formality of the presentation, the make up of the audience and who will be presenting it.Any presentation script, regardless of complexity is like any other business correspondence. It should consist of the same four basic parts, an opening, body, summary and closing.

— *The opening*: The opening of the presentation sets the stage for what is to follow. Participants are introduced and the purpose of the presentation is stated. You should also present a VERY BRIEF summary or outline of the points to be covered. This helps keep your audience oriented properly within the framework of your script.

— *Body*: This is the part of the script in which the bulk of the subject matter is presented. The body of a long presentation should be separated into smaller, easily assimilated modules. Each module or sub-section should make a single point or convey one idea. These sub-sections should each have their own simple opening, body and summary.

— *Summary*: This portion should be very brief and simple. Here is your chance to reinforce the central theme and purpose of your presentation.

There is an old axiom that says ... "Tell them what you are going to tell them, tell them, and then tell them what you told them." This pretty well sums it up.

Question and answer sessions often follow a final summary and are very productive if managed properly. You should encourage questions from the audience if time or format permits, but be prepared to answer them. If you do not know the correct answer to a question, don't try to fake it. You should refer the question to someone who can answer it correctly or make a note to yourself to obtain the answer later. When you do, contact the person or persons who asked it as soon as possible. This makes an excellent door opener for follow up calls.

— *Old speakers trick:* If you Don't want any questions, look the audience over and ask if there are any questions. This puts pressure on the audience and makes many of them choke, and therefore, not respond.

— *Closing:* In a well structured closing, points raised during the question and answer session (if any) are summarised and any handout material that was not required during the presentation is distributed. Handout material which emphasizes each key point or idea permits your audience to review the subject and assures that your words will remain fresh in their minds. Handout material should not be distributed before a presentation unless it is critical to the theme since it invariably leads to audience distraction.

6. Select the proper visual aids

With the script developed and the audience research completed, this decision should be simple. A five minute presentation to a three person audience is probably best made with handout material alone, or even simple flip charts. Larger audiences might be effectively reached by using a few simple overhead transparencies. (yes, they still have their purpose)

7. Prepare a story board

A story board does not have to be complicated or time consuming to prepare. Its main purpose is to give a general view of the presentation and communicate the important items to the technicians and artists who are creating and assembling the images.

You can make your story board using file cards and post- it notes, or opt for a comprehensive color story board, prepared by professional designers. Changes at the story board level are relatively inexpensive since no images have been produced. During the story board phase you can rehearse the script and easily rearrange, revise, delete from and add to your presentation. When your story board reaches final form it becomes the finished draft for your presentation. This is one of the most important design tools used to produce your graphics.

The final story board should consist of a sketch of each individual image, in sufficient detail to convey its approximate finished appearance. If more detailed instructions are needed to create an image than can be clearly conveyed on the story board, individual layout sheets should be prepared. These sheets should specify colors, formats, fonts and values for graphs and charts.

If specific artwork or photographs must be used in an image, they should be clearly indicated on the story board or layout sheet for that image.

8. Produce the visuals

With careful, timely planning, the only task remaining is mechanical process of production. The complete and accurate planning that you have done to this point assures a smooth production cycle without the need for unnecessary last minute changes. This is true whether you use Magic Markers to prepare flip charts on a newsprint pad or require a nine projector slide presentation with live video.

Today's computer graphics products permit you to make changes and alterations that could not be accomplished using any other method of production. While last minute changes are possible, avoiding them can still help cut the cost of your presentation by eliminating revision and rush fees.

9. Rehearse—rehearse—rehearse

Your final script and outline or story board permit you to rehearse your presentation even before the visuals are completed. This assures that when your final images are prepared and ready, you will be as well. If you'd like to really test your mettle, drag out the camcorder and tape your rehearsal.

10. Presentation day

On the day of the presentation, arrive and set up early.

Have spare projector bulbs and extra copies of the handout material close at hand. You have your visuals, you are well rehearsed, the room is set up and the participants are all prepared. Speak clearly and with authority. A little humor if tastefully added can help break the tension of the moment. There should be no surprises. Make certain that the audience questions have been addressed, and of course, thank everyone for attending.

11. Follow up

Check back with the attendants and participants to assure that your presentation goals were met. A questionnaire distributed at the end of your presentation can be a source of critical information for follow up calls or future presentations. Encourage the attendants to call or write with any questions that they did not get answered during the presentation.

Harmful Sins of Visual Presentation

The illegible image

Images not clearly seen by the entire audience add confusion and distraction. If you have to say "I know you can't read this but.....," why include the visual at all? The more eagle-eyed viewers may take exception to this attack on their literacy while others are attempting to see what is on the screen. While straining to read the visual, they cannot be expected to be paying full attention to what is being said.

One popular rule of thumb is the *"8H" rule of legibility.* In a nutshell, if you can read an image from eight times its height, odds are your audience will be able to read it when projected. As an example.... You have a flip chart which is 2 feet high. If you can read the chart from 16 feet away, that chart will probably be legible when converted to a slide or overhead transparency. 35 millimeter slides are about an inch in height. If you can read a slide from 8 inches distance, that slide will be legible under most presentation conditions.

The useless image

Images should be designed to please the mind as well as the eye of the viewer. If an image has no specific place or purpose in a presentation other than "it is pretty", it should probably be removed.

The overly complex image

More images with fewer ideas on each are better than a few images which are complicated or difficult to understand. A single idea or set of facts per image, timed to the speaker's pace will add punch and emphasis to each important idea assuring maximum retention. Most people are easily bored, and one generally accepted rule of thumb states that if an image remains on the screen longer than 7 to 10 seconds, you begin to lose viewer attention.

Chartjunk

Closely related to the previous deadly sin, *"chartjunk"* is a phrase coined to identify confusing elements which really have no place on the image. Many presenters insist on having a glaring coloured logo in the corner of every image. While a common element can add continuity to a presentation, blazing logos and distracting objects can detract from the message — after all, isn't the message what it's all about?

Chartoons

A first cousin to chartjunk, *"chartoons"* are overly cute attempts to make a presentation appear more professional by adding lots of distracting, tacky, aggravating symbols and such. These usually appear right after a presenter has discovered a clip art library.

Ransom note design

Just because you have access to 35 fonts does not mean that you are required to use them. A single font throughout an entire presentation is usually quite sufficient. Use bold, italic, underline, quotations and/or color changes to emphasize or subdue key points or words.

Calico or crazy quilt graphics

Keep the colours to a minimum. A single background colour throughout a presentation lends an air of continuity. You can separate broad sections of a presentation by changing background colours, but keep the changes to a minimum. Unless your purpose is to shock or grab serious attention, try to keep all background colours within the same color family.

Mixed visual metaphors

You should not mix your metaphors when you speak, so please don't mix them in your graphics without specific purpose. You would not use warm colors in an image whose subject was ice hockey unless you wanted to emphasise the warm comfortable environment of the arena.

2

PLANNING FOR A BETTER PRESENTATION

The most common ways to make others aware of your work is by publishing the results in a journal article, or by giving an oral or poster presentation (often at a regional or national meeting). While efforts are made to teach the elements of writing a journal article in many graduate school curricula, much less attention is paid to teaching those skills necessary to develop a good oral or poster presentation—even though these arguably are the most common and most rapid ways to disseminate new findings. In addition, the skills needed to prepare an oral presentation can be used in a variety of other settings—such as preparing a seminar in educational institutions, organising a dissertation defence, conducting a job interview seminar, or even addressing potential philanthropic sources.

Effective oral communication is an important—but often overlooked and underpracticed—skill in scientific and academic endeavours. The principles should be applied whenever you are faced with making a public presentation, whether it's a journal club presentation or a more formal talk, such as a conference presentations, job talks, and invited seminars.

There are very few people having a natural talent for delivering outstanding presentations. On the other hand, foresight, hard work, and practice can carry most of the rest of us into the 'very good' level of presentation skills. The standards for public speaking in the scientific and academic realms are relatively low, so a good presentation often is memorable. I've attempted to compile a short summary of skills needed to make a good presentation so that a user can learn these skills with a little effort and practice, then apply them in professional settings.

INITIAL PLANNING

This is where you begin to tailor the talk to the situation, and for that reason this stage is very important for a successful presentation. Talk to your host and clarify these points before you spend much preparation time. If the environment and audience are unfamiliar to you, this is a critical stage. You may even want to do a literature search on potential audience members to identify areas of common interest or potential questions which may arise. Begin this stage early—the more lead time you allow yourself, the more time you will have to think up novel approaches to the topic and the more interesting and substantial your presentation will be.

Before you begin preparing the presentation, you'll need to determine:

The type of talk you will be expected to give:

- — Will this be an informal chat, a seminar discussion, or a more formal presentation?
- — Different talks have different purposes; the intent of a conference presentation is not the same as a job talk. When in doubt, ask for guidance from your host.

The Composition of the Audience

- — Will you be speaking to a general audience or specialists?
- — How many people are expected to attend?
- — Is this likely to be a friendly audience? An interactive audience?

The Time Allotted for the Talk

- — The longer the talk, the more freedom you will have to explore the topic
- — A short talk needs to be very clear and to address the topic directly.
- — Is question time included?

Expectations for Information Content

- — Is there a specific purpose for having you give a talk? Clarify the expectations beforehand and plan to address them during the presentation.
- — Will you be presenting novel concepts to this audience, or building upon their prior knowledge? Either way, make sure you cover the basics clearly, and early in the talk, to avoid loosing the audience.

PREPARATION

Once you have a general idea of what you want to say, you'll have to decide how to say it. Unlike a conversation or a written document, a talk is a one-shot attempt to make a point. By contrast, a conversation consists of repetitions and clarification's based on questions and immediate feedback, while a written paper allows a reader to puzzle through its contents as often as necessary. It is essential that your talk be well-constructed and tidy, and that your points be presented to the audience both a logical sequence and unambiguously. This all takes a fair amount of preparation. Start early!

Here are a few pointers to get you started:

— Start preparing far in advance by thinking through what needs to be said. Collect material which may relate to the topic from unusual sources, and sleep on these ideas. The final product will be more fully-developed and interesting.

— Using big letters and a bold pen, write a clear statement of the problem and its importance, and then pin that statement on the wall above your desk.

— Develop this theme into one jargon-free sentence that will catch the attention of the audience. Next, identify the issues you plan to address.

— Arrange these issues in a logical sequence (which may change as you develop the talk). This process is easier if you use index cards to organise your talk, with one idea per card.

— Computer-based presentation programs (PowerPoint, Persuasion, etc.) can be wonderful time-savers. The time invested in learning to use these programs is rewarded by the speed with which a presentation can be created, even by a moderately-skilled user. These programs are good tools for organising your presentation (an electronic version of the index cards idea), they can be used to create visuals for the presentation (e.g., slides and transparencies), and even project those visuals during the presentation.

— Avoid using lists (First ..., Second ...); you may confuse listing systems (First ..., Point B..., and another thing ...), or you may discover later in the talk that you've missed a point entirely, and then you'll be forced to backtrack. Both of these problems tend to distract your audience away from the points you are trying to make, and both give the appearance of poor organisational skills.

— Retention of information by the audience is reduced as a talk proceeds, so if you do want to make a series of points, organise them from the most to the least important. That way, the audience is more likely to remember the important points later. You may even find that the less important points become irrelevant to the focus of the talk as you practice.

— Determine transition elements which will help your audience to follow the link from one issue to the next. These should be logical, and may presented by posing a question, or explaining your own discovery of the link's existence.

— Use short sentences with simple constructions. The concept will be made more clear, and the sentence structure is more similar to conversational styles.

— Run through the talk once, early. Go back and re-think the sequencing. Discard non-essential elements.

— Don't assume the audience will be familiar with basic concepts that form the foundation of your talk. Outline these concepts briefly but clearly early in the talk to avoid confusion.

— Attempt to identify problems or questions the audience may have and address them in the talk, before the audience has a chance to think of these things themselves.

— Determine which elements would benefit by being presented with visual aids. Spend time working out the best way to present the material. Head on over to the accompanying tutorials for information on presenting material in an effective way using visual aids.

— Prepare thumbnails sketches of these visual aids, then run through the talk again. Re-work the most appropriate and essential visual aids and discard the rest. Don't forget to proof-read your visuals! Do so while there is plenty of time to re-print that critical slide with the glaring typo.

— The earlier you start on the visuals, the better they will be. On the other hand, avoid fine tuning each visual endlessly; if you find yourself diddling the details, go on to do something more productive instead.

— When in doubt about which presentation medium to use (transparencies, slides, videos, multimedia, etc.), choose the format which is the least complex which remains consistent with both clarity and content of the presentation. Keep in mind that the more technology you use, the more things there will be which can go wrong. These technological difficulties may develop into a gruesome presentation experience, particularly if you are giving the talk in an unfamiliar setting!

— If you do need to use multimedia technology in your presentation, call ahead to make sure the technology you require is supported in the room where you'll be talking!

— The most important preparation factor is to Rehearse! Do so in private at first. Then for a real acid test, videotape yourself and watch the results with a critical eye. It's often a painful and humbling experience, but the results will be worth it.

— You can then try the presentation out in front of a few colleagues. Ask for feedback, then *act on that information*. Select those who know a little about your topic, and not those who know a lot. This will focus your attention on attempting to explain why you did what you did in simple terms, rather than encouraging attention to details only specialists care about.

— If you start preparing early, you'll have plenty of time to refine the presentation based on your colleagues' feedback. This is always a useful process.

— Don't waste your colleagues' time; if you are sincere about wanting that feedback, don't wait until the night before the presentation to ask for other people's input.

— Remember, the shorter the talk, the more difficult it will be to cover the material clearly and completely. Be strict about including only what is essential information for the presentation, and removing *all* the non-essential tidbits.

Outlining

The primary purpose of a presentation is to provide information which the audience will then remember at a later date. Detailed referencing of material or extensive review of data won't be remembered—and may put the audience to sleep!

One way to maintain interest is to organise and present the material in a novel manner. Using a non-standard ordering of material will help to keep the audience interested. Similarly, organising your material in a new way (rather than re-working an old talk) will help to keep your own interest in the topic, and will result in a talk which is more fresh and exciting.

The importance of outlining is often stressed in preparing written and oral presentations, but an outline following a linear format (headings, subheadings, etc.) may be restrictive. A list of terms and ideas can be daunting, and tends to focus attention on the final items. Consider creating an 'idea network' as an alternative approach for organising your presentation.

A question that often is asked at this stage is "Is this enough material for the talk?". Actually, you'll probably find that you have far too much material. It is important to develop a realistic view of how much material is appropriate, and the ability to be ruthless in eliminating non-essential material. These abilities vary widely among presenters, and are important factors in determining the quality of the presentation.

Practice Makes Perfect

You've probably heard this before, but that doesn't diminish its importance. Practice is the single most important factor contributing to a good presentation. No matter how rushed you might be, make time for at least a few practice runs. The effects of practice will be apparent, and a poorly presented talk reflects upon both you and your attitude towards the material and audience. Don't be fooled by people who claim to be able to throw together a talk at a moment's notice. Generally, their talks fall into two categories—talks which are disjointed and awkward, and talks which have had the rough edges removed by numerous prior presentations (i.e., dull and unexciting).

One problem is that you can waste a tremendous amount of time by practicing all the wrong parts of your talk. It is necessary to run through the talk a few times to get an idea of how the talk will flow. After that, seek some outside feedback to make sure you are on the right track. Finally, practice all parts of the talk equally. If you always start at the beginning and work until you run into problems, the beginning of the talk will be great, but the final portion of the talk will be relatively more weak. Begin one out of every few practice runs in the middle or at the end of the talk.

PRESENTATION

Having spent all that time preparing the talk itself, there are still a few things you can do at the last minute which will help ensure a successful presentation.

— Before the day begins, or last thing the night before, run through your talk once more. Use a mirror or visualise standing in front of an audience as you practice. If you've brought a slide carousel with you (a good idea), check their arrangement. You probably won't have time to do this later.

— If possible, take a tour the room you'll use for the presentation early in the day. Look for potential problems with line of sight due to furniture, dark spots due to dead overhead lights, intruding sound from ventilation—these all can be fixed with a bit of prior warning and a polite request.

— If you need specialised equipment, make sure it is available ahead of time—don't spring that information on your host at the last minute.

— Check again to see that your slides are oriented properly in the carousel. Lock that ring!

— Make sure the focus switch works, and determine who will be controlling the slide advance. Do the slide advance, reverse, and focus features all work?

— It's your show, so ask for help with the equipment if you need it; it's better to ask for help then fumble around during the presentation. Determine who will be controlling equipment for you.

Computer presentations introduce a whole host of potential issues—here are a few to consider:

— Is the host software compatible with your presentation? Are the fonts, bullets, colours, etc. the same?

— Is there a sound card in the host computer? Is the sound system operational—but not too painfully loud?

— Back-up your presentation before you leave using an alternate medium, then bring it with you separately from the one you plan to use (e.g., packed in a different suitcase), or e-mail it to yourself as an attachment—you may be able to access it from your destination if needed.

— Alternatively, e-mail it to your host and ask that her or she download the file and test it on the computer you'll be using—before you depart for the trip!

— Did you include all the required files and resources for your presentation?

— You might consider making a set of 35mm presentation slides from your electronic presentation, then bringing the stack of slides along as your fail-safe backup—this strategy may depend upon your degree of compulsiveness and/or paranoia, or how important the presentation is to you.

— Keep in mind that failures of technology can be devestating, but that (1) the embrassment is greater on the part of the host if their equipment is at fault, and (2) the host is usually impressed if you provide an alternate solution to the problem—suggesting you are a proactive and prepared person.

— Irrespective of what your presentation medium might be, letting your presentation slides, disk, CD, etc. out of your sight before the presentation begins can lead to disaster.

— If the room is large, or your voice small, use a microphone. Try it out before the audience arrives (blowing into the mike or counting '1-2-3' they have arrived is tacky, so don't do it).

— Check to see that accessories are present; chalk, eraser, markers, and especially a pointer. If it is a laser pointer, does it have fresh batteries loaded? Keep in mind that green wavelength lasers DEVOUR batteries!

— Avoid standing behind a lectern or desk during the presentation. Stand to one side of the projection screen or blackboard, and closer to the audience if possible.

— Moderate movement and hand gestures are OK, but avoid pacing and flapping.

— Don't be afraid to insist on a few minutes to yourself prior to the talk; 15 to 30 minutes is standard. If you have an itinerary, check to see that you've had time allotted for preparation. If you are running behind, see if someone is willing to meet with you after the talk, then use that time to prepare instead. Use this time to double-check your materials, and your introductory and summary statements. Don't allow yourself to be distracted by audience members coming up to chat.

— Don't wait until the very last minute to make that run to the bathroom, and remember to check carefully your appearance—including zippers, buttons and other closures—before you reappear.

The Moment of Truth

Gulp. So you are sitting there, about to be introduced. Now what?

Take several deep breaths as you are being introduced (but don't sigh!). Visualise your rehearsed opening statement; don't improvise at the last moment.

State your objectives at start of your talk, then restate them again at the end of the talk. In between, discuss how your material relates to these objectives.

Unless you intentionally have had experience as a stand-up comic, avoid making jokes. The results can be disappointing, and may suggest an unprofessional attitude.

Choose a natural, moderate rate of speech and use automatic, moderate gestures.

Monitor your behaviour, and avoid habitual behaviours (pacing, fumbling change in pocket, twirling hair).

Laser pointers are wonderful pointing devices, but remember not to point them at the audience. They are best used by flashing the pointer on and off, so that the place you are indicating is illuminated briefly. Don't swirl the laser around and around one place on the projection screen, or sweep it from place to place across the screen. This is very distracting for the audience, and they will end up watching the pointer and not listening to what you are saying.

Likewise, and for the same reasons, avoid using the cursor as in pointer in your computer presentations.

Also try to avoid pointing things out on the computer's monitor at the podium—although the presenter's natural tendency is to concentrate on the monitor's screen, the audience will be looking over your shoulder at the projection screen and won't be able to see where your finger is pointing. If you find yourself doing this, power-off or disable the monitor to force yourself to concentrate on the projection screen.

Enthusiasm for your topic is contagious, but don't overdo it—you'll alienate the audience.

Converse with your audience. Involve them in the process of the presentation by posing questions and making eye contact. Be patient if you ask a question—answers sometimes take time to formulate.

Keep an eye on your time, and don't run over your limit. Ever.

Be prepared for interruptions (late arrivals, cell phones or pagers, burned out projector bulbs, fire drills, etc.).

If you must turn down the room lights, don't turn them off entirely. Don't leave the lights down any longer than necessary—remember to turn them back up! Of course, the snores from the sleeping audience may remind you to turn the lights back on if you've forgotten.

Don't apologise for any aspect of your presentation. This should be your very best effort; if you have to apologise, you haven't done your job properly.

Don't criticise aspects of the trip, city, facilities, etc. during your talk. This is another way to alienate your audience quickly. For instance, they may or may not have chosen to live in this horrible climate, but it isn't your place to remind them how horrible it is. Remember that you are a guest and it is impolite to exhibit your prejudices publically.

Strive to have a prepared and memorable summary. If nothing else, the take home message is what the audience will remember after you leave.

When you reach the summary and are about to finish, resist the temptation to add a few last impromptu words.

They will be unpracticed, and will be the last thing many of your audience will hear you say. End your talk with the insightful, firm summary statement you have prepared.

Don't be afraid to give yourself credit for your own work, but do remember to give others credit where due. If planned for later in the talk, don't forget to acknowledge these people's efforts, even if you have to skip a statement or two to remain within your time frame. The best friend of one of these contibutors may be in your audience! If you include slides borrowed from other people, or slides which include other people's data or figures, always give credit to these people right on that slide. This shows a professional attitude, and (better yet) can save you many words of explanation.

Prepare for the Questions

Your presentation doesn't end once you've finished what you have to say. The question period often is the part of the talk which influences the audience the most. After all, you've had time to practice the rest of the talk. This is the part of the presentation where your ability to interact with the audience will be evaluated. Since you can't always predict the what you'll be asked, how can you prepare for the questioning? Here are a few guidelines:

— Always repeat each question so the entire audience knows what you've been asked.

— Before you answer, take a moment to reflect on the question. By not rushing to give an answer, you show a degree of respect for the questioner, and you give yourself time to be sure you are answering the question that actually was asked. If you are unsure, restate the question or ask for a clarification.

— Above all, wait for the questioner to finish asking the question before you begin your answer! The only exception is when it becomes necessary to break in on a vague, rambling question; this is your show, and you have only a limited time to make your presentation. It is essential, however, that you break in tactfully. Say something like "So, are you asking ....?" This will focus the question and give you a place to begin an answer. Remember that your ability to interact with an audience also is being evaluated.

— If a question is asked during the talk, and it will clarify an ambiguity, answer it immediately.

— Postpone questions aimed at resolving specific problems (or arcane knowledge) until the end of the talk, or private discussion. This is particularly important if the answer will distract either you or the audience away from the flow of your presentation.

— Avoid prolonged discussions with one person, extended answers, and especially arguments.

If you can't answer a question, just say so. Don't apologise. You then may:

— Offer to research an answer, then get back to the questioner later.

— Suggest resources which would help the questioner to address the question themselves.

— Ask for suggestions from the audience.

Finish your answer by asking the person who asked that question whether or not you answered the question sufficiently for them. This acknowledges and thanks the questioner, it lets the rest of the audience feel comfortable asking questions (because it shows you are genuinely interested in addressing audience issues, not just in lecturing to them), and it gives you a chance to more fully answer the question if your first effort was not quite on target. If the questioner says you didn't answer it and you believe you did, either ask them to clarity the question or suggest that the two of you go into more detail at a break or after the presentation.

Hints for Efficient Practice

Read through thes text before you begin. For the first few tries, and again for the last few, stand in front of a mirror but far enough back so you can see your head and feet. Work at being relaxed. Stand with feet slightly apart and one foot slightly forward to prevent swaying and weight shifts. Hold your notes in one hand, with the other held naturally at your side. This posture will seem awkward, but looks natural and relaxed. Practice it.

Breath slowly and deeply, and speak from your diaphragm; project your voice. Practice making eye contact with your imaginary audience, but don't single out one individual (a real person eventually will notice your attention, and end up squirming in their seat).

Don't procrastinate when you actually are ready to practice. Take two deep breaths, then begin. Avoid looking at your notes when you don't need to do so. Watch your reflection in the mirror as you speak, looking for odd and distracting habits.

Your words will probably be different each time you practice, but do try to stick to the general outline of your notes. Don't attempt to memorise your text; use your notes only as reference points to keep you on track. Think about the ideas, and your words will follow naturally. Speak slowly and clearly, and use gestures.

A tape recorder or videotape are the most useful tools for feedback. Look for variations in speed or tone, or for the dreaded 'um's (and those cousins, the 'er's, 'like's and 'you know's). Again, look for distracting mannerisms—don't pace, twirl your hair, or adjust your clothing. Make sure you are speaking to your audience, not to the floor, ceiling, or projection screen. Don't hide behind the lecturn.

What you say should be readily understandable by the audience. Pay strict attention to diction; it is essential that you speak clearly and distinctly. If you have a regional or foreign accent you should be careful to speak even more slowly. Check often to be sure that your audience understands and is following what you are saying. It isn't necessary to attempt to eliminate your accent. On the other hand, rightly or wrongly, there is little room in professional presentations for regional or cultural dialects.

Listen carefully to the words you use, not to what you *think* you are saying. Are these the best words for making your point? Are they unambiguous? Avoid using jargon whenever possible.

Using Notes

A prepared series of notes can be useful, particularly if you get off track during a presentation. Keep in mind that most people find that the notes aren't really needed once you get to the final talk. Poorly constructed notes, on the other hand, can impede a presentation. Here are some hints on preparing effective notes.

Begin by determining the underlying concept of the talk, then decide on the minimum essential material needed to support that concept. Working from an outline, write out the talk and practice it once or twice. Reorganise the material so the talk flows more evenly, rephrase your statements as needed, and use a pencil to highlight key phrases.

Run through the talk again with a pencil and paper nearby. Refer only to the key phrases to recall the talk's content. If you run into problems, jot down the problem with the pencil and paper, then continue. When finished, review your notes and comments. Rework the talk by incorporating your comments, removing unneeded words (or entire sections), and include comments or symbols to remind yourself of upcoming items (a new slide, a joke, an important item).

Run through the talk again, writing comments as you go. Transcribe the keywords, etc. onto index cards. Write out the first few sentences of your introduction only. If necessary, you can then use these sentences as a springboard to get into the rest of the talk. Otherwise, the cards should contain only the keywords and reminders you've developed for this talk.

Write across the short dimension and on only one side of each card, keeping the bottom 1/3 of the card blank. Use the blank space for later comments or references, and for numbering the cards in a final sequence. Use a subdued color of card instead of a conspicuous white card; they will be less distracting for the audience during the real talk. Practice again a few times making modifications, then punch a hole through the bottom left corner of the card and string the cards in sequence onto a clasp ring.

3

PREPARING YOUR CONTENT

COMPONENTS OF CONTENT

Action

Before you ever begin writing a presentation, you need to answer this question: What do you want your audience to do? Whether it's selling your product, securing a new business client, or promoting your favourite organisation, every presentation is based upon moving an audience to perform an "action". At times, the action may simply be gaining enough information to enable them to do something else. In any case, every presenter should be able to write (in 15 words or less) what he wants the audience to do as a result of his presentation. It is important to keep this action to 15 words or less to truly define and narrow the action.

Body

Once you have determined the "audience action", the next step is to construct the main points of your presentation. These points should promote and convince your audience to perform the desired action. Because audience members typically only recall a few key points of a presentation, it is a good idea to limit content to 5 key points. And each of these key points should relate directly to the desired action.

Conclusion

The conclusion should summarise your key points, and most importantly, tell your audience what "action" they need to perform. Make sure the ending is clear, concise, and to the point.

Opening

The opening should grab your audience's attention and get them excited about your presentation. In addition, the opening should tell your audience why they are there, why they should listen to you, and what they will gain from your presentation.

Editing Your Content

When you have finished writing your presentation draft, you will surely edit it for misspellings and grammatical errors. But those revisions come later . . . Before you ever get to that state, take a look at your work to make sure it packs the punch you want it to. Try the following tips:

Use descriptive words

Consider the following passage:

> We are pleased to announce that our team finished the project ahead of schedule. Though the project seemed like it would certainly be delayed, thanks to the efforts of Rahul Agnihotri, it was not.

This passage provides the facts, but the fire is missing. The descriptions that make people want to "sit up and listen" are curiously absent. Consider the revised passage:

We are thrilled to say "WE DID IT!" Against what seemed like a mountain of obstacles, we finished the project 4 days ahead of schedule. Special kudos are in order to Rahul Agnihotri who contributed Herculean effort to push this thing out the door.

Use active voice

The battle between active and passive is commonplace. The key to powerful writing is using the active voice the majority of the time.

Passive

The results of last quarter's sales have been compiled and are to be presented at the next sales meeting.

Active

We have compiled last quarter's sales figures and will present them at the next sales meeting.

Avoid jargon

In USA, Corporate America is currently besieged by the need to use jargon and double-talk. Boardrooms around the country spin with terms like leverage, multi-task, facilitate, utilise, etc. These words turn the simple into complicated and the clear into muddled. Perhaps you need to toss around these terms at times, but these words have no place in presentations. Resist the temptation to use ambiguous jargon when straightforward diction will do.

Communication Pitfalls

Once your content message is complete and you have the

draft of "what" you want to say, its time to put your message into language your audience can understand. By eliminating the common pitfalls below, you can ensure your audience understands your message.

Pretentiousness

Remember that as a presenter it is your job to inform, not to impress! Avoid creating communication barriers by using formal or "big" words. These inflated words often make you appear less credible than you may well be. Remember, keeping it simple is usually the best approach.

Emulate	Imitate
Inculcate	Teach
Valiant	Brave

Triteness

In order to create the greatest impact for your message, avoid cliches and other trite phrases. Use words that express your ideas without relying on other's expressions to communicate your message. Your message is most powerful when it's in your own words.

— Life is what you make it

— There are two sides to every question

— The crack of dawn

— Tower of strength

Jargon

Before you use any type of corporate or cultural jargon, make sure you understand your audience. If you can, avoid using jargon altogether. The easiest way to lose an audience is to throw around words that mean nothing.

CSR	Customer Service Representative
VAR	Value Added Reseller
SME	Subject Matter Expert
ISP	Internet Service Provider

Misused Words

The spoken word can be quite different from the written word. Many things that we allow to fly in speech simply look like glaring errors once they are written on a handout or an overhead. Below are several commonly misused words and their correct usage.

Ago vs. Since

Both words speak of the past, and they are often used interchangeably. However, these words have different meanings. Ago carries the mind from the present to the past. Since carries the mind from the past to the present.

Correct

— It was almost 25 years ago that they were married.

— It is (or has been) almost 25 years since they got married.

Since vs. Because

Since is related to time. Because is related to cause.

Incorrect

— Since the Dodgers are so far behind, we are leaving the game early.

Correct

— Because the Dodgers are so far behind, we are leaving the game early.

Even Better

— We are leaving the game early because the Dodgers are so far behind.

Compare to vs. Compare with

— "Compare to" is used to liken two things or to put them in the same category.

— The economy can be compared to a stallion charging at the gate.

— "Compare with" is used to place two things side by side for the purpose of examining their similarities or differences.

— The American economy can be compared with the European economy to note how military history impacts future economics.

Among vs. Between

Between is used correctly when there are two items involved. Among means in the midst of countable things. When the things are not countable, the correct word is "amid" or "amidst".

Incorrect

— She is standing among the boys.

— Masked firemen groped among the wreckage hours later. Note that "wreckage" is not countable.

Correct

— She is standing between the boys.

— Masked firemen groped amidst the wreckage hours later.

Note about Between

A single noun that follows "between" becomes plural. Consider the following: The product is currently between first and second releases.

Comprise

Comprise means to contain, embrace, or include. So, the whole comprises the parts — not the reverse.

Incorrect:

— Parts A, B, and C comprise the product.

Correct

— The product comprises Parts A, B, and C.

Disinterested vs. Uninterested

Disinterested means one is neutral and has no personal interest in the outcome of a situation. Uninterested means one is lacking interest. The key to using these words correctly is asking "does the party have a selfish interest in the outcome, where or not he is interested?" If he does, "uninterested" is the correct word to use.

Correct

— Up to now, the Sales team has been uninterested in the revenue figures because the Accounting group has been reworking the compensation packages.

In Order To

Generally this prepositional phrase can be eliminated. Consider the following sentences:

— She wants to go to college in order to become a teacher.

— She wants to go to college to become a teacher.

Quote vs. Quotation

Quote is a verb. Quotation is a noun. Nevertheless, it is now quite commonplace to use the word "quote" as both a noun and a verb.

Incorrect

— The VP of Sales and Marketing gave a quote to the press . . .

Correct

— The reporter quoted the VP of Sales and Marketing . . .

USING ABBREVIATIONS CORRECTLY

People use abbreviations everyday. In general, no one gives them a second thought. That is, no one gives them a second thought — until these abbreviations appear 4" tall on a projection screen. At that point, you may second-guess your grammatical confidence. Follow these guidelines to be sure to use the correct abbreviations in your next presentation.

Titles and Ranks

— Mr., Mrs., Ms., and Dr. are abbreviated when used before a name. Note that Miss is not an abbreviation. Examples: Ram Krishan, Gita Verma.

— Civil and military titles are abbreviated only when

used before a full name. If only the last name is used, it must be preceded by the full title.

Correct	*Incorrect*
Lt. Gov. Rakesh Sinha	Lt. Gov. Sinha
Sgt. Ramesh Saxena	Sgt. Saxena

— When used after full names, Jr. and Sr. are abbreviated. Example: Sachin Joshi, Jr., and Romesh Powar, Sr.

Titles and Certifications

— Scholarly degrees are abbreviated. Note that title, name, and degree cannot be combined.

Correct	*Incorrect*
Anand Sharma, Ph.D.	Dr. Anand Sharma, Ph.D.

Time Designations

— Such designations as A.M., P.M., EST, and IST are always abbreviated. Note that A.M. and P.M. require the period, but EST and IST do not.

Acronyms and Familiar Initials

The full forms of initials pronounced as words are rarely written as words (WWW, ZIP, COBOL). Additionally, those entities known better by their familiar initials (IRS, FBI, CBI, NFC) are best abbreviated.

Using Good Reasoning

There are two common types of reasoning that form the basis of content development. These two types of reasoning are deductive and inductive logic. As a presenter, you should examine your content as well as the "action" you want your audience to take. Then, based upon these two items, you should be able to select the reasoning strategy to use in your content development.

Deductive Format

This is the most popular format for presentations. The deductive format is based on a structured lecture. The presenter simply presents his content and recommendations for actions. This direct method does not allow for an abundance of audience participation. Usually questions are limited and held until the end of a presentation.

Deductive example

When using the inductive format, the presenter encourages the audience to come to a logical conclusion on their own. This type of presentation is recommended when you want group dialogue and participation. The presenter usually offers issues, examples, and factual information, and leads a group discussion to come to a logical conclusion.

Inductive Format

When using the inductive format, the presenter encourages the audience to come to a logical conclusion on their own. This type of presentation is recommended when you want group dialogue and participation. The presenter usually offers issues, examples, and factual information, and leads a group discussion to come to a logical conclusion.

Inductive example

The salesperson shows his customer a model of a fast engine and transmission and a set of wide tires. He explains that these components are found in the fastest cars around. Then he shows the customer the car with these parts on it. The customer comes to the conclusion that this car is probably one of the fastest around. By showing the parts that make a car very fast, the sales person allows the customer to come to the conclusion that a car with all those parts must be very fast. This is an inductive presentation.

Mixed Format

There are some instances when you may want to use both forms of reasoning. For example, you may want the group to come to a consensus on a particular issue. Based on the audience's conclusion, you may suggest the recommended course of action to take. This format is the most complicated and takes real planning to execute well.

Brainstorming with Sticky Notes

You know your topic, your audience, and the "call to action". You have tons of great ideas for your presentation. Now it's time to crank up the PowerPoint and get this presentation done . . . Well, not exactly.

Many presenters fall into a classic mistake: they don't adequately develop the presentation content before they begin to make their slides. By no means do you have to flush out every detail, but you should have a solid outline (including opening, key points, closing, and "call to action") before you begin to worry about slides. If you don't have enough information, before you worry about visuals, you may end up concentrating too much effort on background colors and not enough effort on the meat of the message.

Have you ever heard the phrase "throw it on the wall and see what sticks"? Well one of the easiest ways to organise your thoughts is by doing just that. Follow the steps below and you'll be organised in no time!

— Grab a stack of "sticky" notes, a marker, and the nearest blank wall.

— Use your sticky notes to brainstorm all of the points/issues/ideas you want to cover in your presentation.

— Don't worry about what they are or if they fit in. Just be sure to keep on idea per "sticky" note.

— After you have finished brainstorming, organise all your thoughts on the wall. Some notes will fall into categories rather easily, while others won't. Some may not even fit at all.

— Each category will probably turn out to be one of your main points.

— When you are finished, check your main points against your "call to action". If any point is unrelated to the direct action, get rid of it.

— Just crank up the PowerPoint and create that winning presentation!

CLOSING OF A PRESENTATIONS

The closing of a presentation is often the most important part. This is the final chance to reiterate the call to action and make a lasting impression. Following are four different types of presentation closings. Select the type of closing based on your presentation content and audience.

Matching Close

This closing is designed to sell the function, features, benefits, and advantages of a product or service. The opening of the presentation defines the desired characteristics. The body demonstrates that the product or service meets those characteristics. And the close summarises the key characteristics and moves the audience to the product or service with the matching characteristics defined in the opening. By getting audience "buy-in" of the defined characteristics in the opening of your presentation, the closing is a "no-brainer" in moving your audience to purchase your product or service that meets the defined characteristics.

The Matching Close

Opening	*Define characteristics desired*
Body	Demonstrate characteristics of product/service.
Closing	Relate how product features/benefits match desired characteristics.

Pyramid Close

Many times a presenter has a substantial number of points to make in a presentation. Unfortunately, audiences only remember three to four main items. By creating a series of "key point" pyramids, presenters can categorise and weight which points are most important. Using a pyramid close, key points are listed at the top of the pyramid and remaining points are listed below.

The Pyramid Close

Opening	*Define key points to discuss*
Body	Describe key points in-depth using defined subpoints.
Closing	Summarise key points and relate call-to-action to those points.

The opening should mention the key points and the body should define the key points in detail. The closing should reinforce/reiterate the key points and move the audience to the call-to-action.

Solution Close

The solution close is designed to show an audience how to solve a complicated problem/issue. This type of closing breaks down a large problem or issue into subcomponents. The presenter's goal is to demonstrate to the audience how each one can be addressed, thus solving the overall problem. The opening of the presentation should define the problem or issue. The body should break down the issue into subcomponents and provide solutions to each. The close should wrap all of the mini-solutions together. This organisation demonstrates that addressing the subcomponents of a problem can solve the main one.

The Solution Close

Opening	*Define key problem/issue*
Body	Define components of issue.
Provide	Solutions to components.
Closing	Summarise how implementing solutions to components solves overall issue/problem.

Future Close

Predicting a successful future can be an excellent way to close a presentation. People like good news. By showing an audience where they are at present, the factors that will affect the future, and how you can help them succeed in this future, you can effectively reach your audience and make a powerful close. The key to this approach is being realistic in what you predict for the future

The opening of this type of presentation should define where the audience is at present. The body of the presentation should outline the facts, figures, and strategy options. The close should make predictions for the future based on the facts and strategy selected.

The Future Close

Opening	*Define current situation*
Body	Outline facts, figures, and strategy options for the future.
Closing	Summarise future predictions based on selected strategy.

DON'T FORGET A PRESENTATION AGENDA

A presentation agenda is one of the items that many presenters forget to create. An agenda is an important tool for a presenter because it enables the presenter to control the flow of the presentation. It also provides the audience with an overview of the activities to be completed and helps them anticipate and retain information.

Agendas can be especially helpful for interdepartmental meetings or long training sessions. If audience members are privy to an agenda prior to a meeting, they can attend the sections of the presentation that specifically relate to them. They can also delegate attendance if unable to attend certain sections themselves. Consider the following tips for presentation agendas.

Agenda Tips

— Distribute an agenda before the meeting, whenever possible.

— Always have the meeting date, starting time, and meeting location at the top of the agenda.

— Provide an overview of key sections.

— Assign specific time frames to each section.

— Allow a few extra minutes for each section.

4

DEVELOPING AN EFFECTIVE ORAL PRESENTATION

Oral presentations can substitute for a portion of the traditional written proposal in competitive negotiated acquisitions and serve the purpose of a briefing. Oral presentations have emerged as one approach offering promise of saving time, staff resources, and money.

Oral presentations provide offerors an opportunity to present information verbally which they would ordinarily provide in writing. Oral presentations eliminate, or greatly reduce, the need for written material, where information can be verbally conveyed more efficiently and effectively. Evaluators can receive information as to the capability of the offeror — generally demonstrating its understanding of the work or describing how the work will be performed — directly from the key members of the offeror's team that will actually perform the work.

It is conducted in real time and permits communication between presenter and evaluator, so it could be in person or via video teleconference, for example. A taped video presentation, therefore, does not constitute an oral presentation. It does not provide the advantages of communicating and exchanging information. If offerors perceive it as an expensive proposition because of the need for professional taping facilities, it could become a barrier to market entry. Small business could be particularly impacted by this.

Whether you use an oral presentation or get everything in writing, the same principles of fairness, impartiality, and good business judgement must be followed.

Clearly, there is nos one best approach for using oral presentations. They can be used in a variety of acquisitions using different contract types. You can design a scheme that best fits the nature of the acquisition and the availability of resources. You must be prepared to commit resources and capable evaluators to this intense and innovative process. Your methodology can include the most appropriate features that can streamline your particular solicitation and source selection. On the other hand, if your design includes inappropriate features because of poor business judgement or an attempt to use a *one size fits all approach,* you will not gain the efficiencies and savings in time and costs that are possible. Worse, you may end up with a failed process that ends in a protest or other litigation.

Oral presentations are most useful when the requirements are clear and complete. They seem to work especially well with performance and functional specifications and statements of work. If you request complex management or technical information, your presenters and evaluators will not be able to effectively use oral presentations.

If you are requesting information to evaluate an offeror's qualifications or understanding of the work, an oral presentation can be an effective tool. A multiple-award task order contract might be a prime candidate in this regard. Usually you will be evaluating the capability and understanding of the offerors for the type of work to be done—exactly the type of information an oral presentation can most effectively provide. The actual work will be specifically defined in each order.

In deciding whether to use oral presentations, you might also consider industry input. Your market research might reveal circumstances that are favourable or unfavourable to its use. Later in the process, you may get feedback from a draft solicitation or a preproposal conference which makes an oral presentation more or less attractive as a part of your source selection.

PLANNING

You first decide and plan on the use of oral presentations when the source selection or evaluation plan is developed. At this point the evaluation factors and subfactors and proposal preparation instructions are determined. This is when you decide if your particular circumstances are appropriate for an oral presentation and how it will be included in your source selection process.

The oral presentation method does present some unusual considerations. Offerors will be presenting information orally instead of in writing. The solicitation must clearly identify the ground rules for conducting oral presentations and include adequate information from which offerors can prepare their proposals.

Evaluation Factors and Subfactors

You decide on the proper discriminators to make the source selection based on your requirements, objectives, perceived risks, and market research. Once the factors and subfactors are selected, then you can decide whether the information required to evaluate the offeror can be reasonably presented orally. Technical and management information are generally the subjects of oral presentations. The factors and subfactors in these areas should be selected to determine how well qualified the offeror is to perform the work, how well the offeror understands the work, and how the offeror will approach the work. In most situations, the oral presentation will be limited to, and directed to, those evaluation factors and subfactors.

Proposal Preparation Instructions

If oral presentations are appropriate, you must notify offerors that oral presentations will be used to evaluate and select the contractor. Highlight this in the solicitation cover letter and/or the Executive Summary.

Likewise, the proposal preparation instructions must contain explicit instructions and guidance regarding the extent and nature of the process that will be used. For instance, the Proposal Preparation Instructions may require the oral presentation to follow a detailed outline which directly relates the information presented to the evaluation factors and subfactors or may direct the order in which material is presented, and may divide the presentation into topics, tasks, or sections.

You may want to give the offeror a *pop quiz* as part of the presentation. If you do, however, you may have to develop variations of your quiz if some offerors are using the same subcontractors so that later presenters don't have a prepared answer. Also, consider if you want the offeror to submit the presentation material (e.g., charts) before the actual presentation. The instructions governing the oral presentation should discourage elaborate presentations or presentation material. You don't want a dog and pony show.

Developing Sound Preparation Instructions

- — Describe the topics that the offeror must address orally and the technical and management factors that must be covered;
- — State the total amount of time that will be available to make the presentation and who must make the presentation;
- — Describe the limitations on Government-offeror interaction during, and, if possible after, the presentation;
- — State whether the presentation will constitute discussions;
- — State whether the presentation will encompass price or cost and fee;
- — Describe the characteristics and arrangement of the presentation site;
- — State the rules governing the use of presentation media;
- — Describe the format and content of presentation documentation, and their delivery;
- — State whether the presentation will be video or audio taped; and
- — State the approximate timeframe when presentations will be made.

Types of Information

Determining the types of information that will be provided orally is extremely important. Trying to collect and evaluate the wrong type of information will not only make the evaluation more difficult, if not impossible, but also slow the process and probably rob you of the benefits of using oral presentations in the first place.

Also, you can create problems later in the process, e.g., in determining the competitive range or in conducting discussions.

Oral presentations can convey information in such diverse areas as: responses to sample tasks and other "tests"; understanding requirements; experience; quality of samples; and transition plans. You cannot fairly collect or evaluate cost/price information, representations and certifications, and personnel resumes orally. Complex and detailed information that will become part of the contract will also be difficult to obtain and evaluate orally. Remember, you can not incorporate oral statements in the contract by reference. Any information that you want to be made part of the contract needs to be put in writing.

Proposal information will consist of both written and oral material. As a rule of thumb, hard data ("facts") regarding an offeror's performance history and contractual commitments should be provided as part of the written information. Soft data (e.g., capability, plans, approaches) can be conveyed accurately and in sufficient detail through oral presentation.

Timing of the Presentation

The question here is when to hear the oral presentation. This timing decision should focus on how the information will be used in the process and how it affects your potential offerors. If you intend to award on the basis of initial proposals, the timing is not so important. If the presentation is going to be part of the competitive range determination, then timing is important and you must be careful to make sure you don't get into *discussions* or *negotiations* before, during, or immediately after the presentation.

Since preparing and presenting an oral presentation involves time and expense, you don't want to require presentations from offerors who aren't likely to be a serious candidate for award. This can be an important consideration with small business. When this is a concern, you may want to hold oral presentations after you have established the competitive range.

PRELIMINARY MATTERS

Selecting the Order of the Presentations

A lottery or drawing lots by the Contracting Officer are most often used to determine the sequence of presentations. The time between the first and the last presentation should be as short as possible to minimise any advantage to the later presenters. The solicitation should spell out how the selection will be made. You must also decide up front whether any rescheduling will be permitted if an offeror requests a change after you have set the schedule. Consider scheduling problems and how many presentations and evaluators are involved.

The Facility

Usually you will want to conduct the presentations at a facility that you can control. This will probably be more convenient for both sides, it helps you guard against surprises, and insures a more level playing field. However, nothing precludes an oral presentation at an offeror's facility. This may be more efficient if site visits, or other demonstrations, are part of the source selection.

Facility Rules of Thumb

— Make it comfortable for both the presenters and the Government evaluators. The room should be large enough to accommodate all of the participants, the recording equipment, lighting, audiovisual aids, and furniture.

— Make it accessible.

— Make it available, if possible, for inspection by the offerors prior to the time set for the actual presentation.

The solicitation should describe the facility and resources available to the offeror. In addition, the solicitation should be clear as to what types of equipment will be available for the presentation, what equipment, if any, should be provided by the offeror, and any prohibitions regarding equipment types and uses. In addition to making the facility available for inspection, you might consider making it available to offerors for a practice session if circumstances warrant. Allowing offerors to get acquainted with the facility will help ensure that it does not detract from the presentation content.

Discussion of Ground Rules

Prior to any presentations, the contracting officer should discuss responsibilities, both during and following the presentation, with all the Government participants. Remind them that an oral presentation is source selection sensitive and that they may not discuss, within or outside the agency, (except among themselves) anything that occurred or was said at a presentation.

You should also go over the guidelines for the scope of questions and information exchanges with offerors during the presentation. Make sure everyone understands that the intent is to encourage the exchange of information. But you also have to ensure that any limits are clearly understood. If you are combining the presentation with discussions, this is less of a problem. If you intend to avoid discussions, you will have to establish clear guidelines such as the Contracting Officer/ Contract Specialist controlling all exchanges during the presentation. You want to avoid too much control and regulation which might inhibit exchanges of information. Good training and experience in this technique will take care of most of these potential problems.

Recording the Presentation

Recording the presentation is not only required, it makes good business sense and has some distinct advantages. A recording permits evaluators to review the presentation to verify information. In the event of a protest or litigation, you will have an exact record of the presentation. Obviously, if you record one, you must record them all and only the Government should be permitted to record the presentation. Several methods, such as videotape, audiotape, or verbatim written transcripts, are available.

If videotaping is to be used, an audiovisual specialist should be used to operate the taping equipment to ensure the quality of the recording. The videotaping facilities should allow for natural behaviour of presenters. If slides or view graphs are used, the camera should view both the podium and screen at the same time.

Microphones should be placed so that all communications can be recorded clearly and at adequate volume. The videotape will become part of the official record, and a copy should be furnished to the offeror. As part of the official record, the recording is considered Source Selection Sensitive and should be treated accordingly. Similar considerations exist when only an audiotape will be recorded. The point is that every effort should be made to avoid letting the recording become the focus of the presentation.

CONDUCTING THE ORAL PRESENTATION

Government Attendance

As a general rule, all of the Government evaluators should be present at every presentation. The Contracting Officer/Contract Specialist must attend and should chair every presentation. Obviously, the Source Selection Authority must decide whether to attend all the presentations or none of them.

Reviewing the Ground Rules

Prior to the presentation, the Contracting Officer/ Contract Specialist should review the ground rules for the presentation with the offeror. You should discuss any restrictions on Government-offeror information exchanges, , information disclosure rules, documentation requirements, and housekeeping items.

If you are using a quiz as part of your evaluation, you also need to discuss the ground rules for that. Can the offeror caucus before answering? Can the offeror contact outside sources by cell phone before responding? Make sure that everyone knows the rules.

Presenters

Presentations should be made by the offeror's key personnel who will perform or personally direct the work being described, such as project managers, task leaders, and other in-house staff. You need to avoid letting the oral presentation become the domain of the professional presenter. This would be another way to increase costs, detract from the advantages of oral presentations, and adversely affect small businesses. This is your opportunity to actually meet and evaluate the people who will be leading or doing the work.

Submitting videotapes or other forms of media in addition to the presentation should be avoided. If there is major subcontracting, members of subcontractor staff should make the relevant presentation. By requiring the oral presentation to cover only useful information and by limiting the amount of time available for the presentation, sales pitches and costs can be minimised.

Time Limit

You have to establish a firm time limit for each presentation in the solicitation. You should also restrict the amount and type of presentation material that an offeror may use during the presentation. You may want to restrict the number of charts or the number of bullets on each chart. There is no *ideal* amount of time to be allotted.

The only indicators to follow are the complexity of the acquisition and your own (or others) experience and lessons learned. If you are planning a question and answer session, you should exclude it from the allotted time for the presentation or set a separate time limit for it. It is not advisable to limit the time for individual topics or sections within the presentation. As with the proposal itself, this detail is the responsibility of the presenter.

Exchanging Information with Offerors

Open communication and dialog between the offeror and the Government are one of the primary benefits to using oral presentations. As indicated previously, the nature and extent of information exchanges between the offeror and the Government evaluation team is an issue that must be met head on. The rules established in regulation regarding exchanges with offerors during the course of the solicitation process must be watched carefully. This can be especially important if you decide to have your presentations before you establish the competitive range or you are contemplating making an award without discussions. You do not want to inadvertently trigger the rules regarding discussions. Establishing the ground rules in the solicitation for exchanges during the presentation and reviewing them before the presentation is a must. However, limiting dialog to questions that merely repeat statements that may not have been heard by the evaluators makes little sense and adds little value in improving the understanding of the offeror's presentation.

On the other hand, if you've already established the competitive range, the oral presentation may be the optimal setting for conducting discussions.

Evaluation of Presentations

Again, there is no firm rule regarding the best time to evaluate the presentation. Generally, the sooner the better. There are many factors to consider: how many presentations there are; how long each presentation is allowed; and how many evaluators are involved. Evaluations can be performed immediately following each presentation. The evaluations could be performed after all of the presentations have been made, possibly after reviewing the videotape again. If you decide to wait, the evaluators should caucus following each presentation to exchange reactions, summarise potential strengths and weaknesses, and verify perceptions and understandings. Using preprinted evaluation forms will help the evaluators collect their thoughts and impressions. These forms will be useful no matter when evaluations are done and will be more useful if the evaluation standards are preprinted on the form. Remember, even if you use preprinted forms, evaluators have to provide the rationale for their conclusions.

Documentation

The solicitation should require that the offeror provide a listing of names and position titles of all presenters and copies of all slides and other briefing materials that will be used. The presentation might be more useful if the materials are provided to the evaluators before the presentation so they can familiarise themselves with the information. These items become part of the official record along with the audio or video tape recording or transcript. The master copy of the tape or transcript should be sealed and securely stored to ensure there would be no allegations of tampering in the event of a protest or court action requiring additional copies to be made. Your ground rules should be clear about how you will treat documents or information referenced in the presentation material but never presented orally. You should also be clear about how you will evaluate material that doesn't comply with your solicitation instructions, such as too many charts or too many bullets per chart. Remember, the object is to communicate information efficiently, effectively, and fairly and to avoid surprises.

ADVANTAGES OF ORAL PRESENTATIONS

Oral presentations have the potential of significantly reducing the time and costs associated with the source selection process. Both sides can benefit from this. Oral presentations can avoid lengthy written marketing pitches and essay writing contests. Some types of written proposal information, particularly technical and management, which are costly to prepare, may be better conveyed and understood when explained orally or demonstrated visually. Oral presentation techniques also allow greater "face-to-face" interaction between buyers and sellers.

Through an oral presentation, evaluators often gain a view of the offeror's key personnel by witnessing how they present themselves, how they work together, and how they communicate technical information to Government personnel. This process provides many of the features of a "job interview" of the proposed key individuals such as the Project Manager. Additionally, the oral presentation process may provide an opportunity to separate offerors who really have the expertise to satisfy the requirement from those offerors who simply know how to write a great proposal.

— Can Save Significant Time;

— Can Improve Communication Between the Government and Offerors;

— Can Reduce Government Evaluations Costs;

— Can Reduce Offerors' Proposal Preparation Costs;

— Can Increase Competition by Reducing Market Entry Barriers;

— Can Improve Ability to Select Most Advantageous Offer.

Practical Hints

— Presenters should not include overly detailed, technical information on slides. Attempting to put a written technical proposal on presentation slides makes it difficult for evaluators to read and follow.

— Ask for briefing materials in advance of the presentation so that it can be reviewed by the evaluators attending the presentation. This will improve the evaluators ability to understand the presentation.

— The setting for the oral presentation should be comfortable and free from disturbance and interruption.

— The proposal preparation instructions should clearly state whether the information in the oral presentation will be used solely for evaluation purposes in selecting the contractor, or whether such information may become part of the contract.

— The Government should not accept any materials that were not actually part of the oral presentation.

— Where time limits or restrictions on the amount of presentation material will be used, such restrictions should be clearly identified in the solicitation.

— Allow sufficient time between presentations to permit the evaluation team to caucus and reach consensus.

— If practicable, evaluate and rate the oral presentations immediately after each presentation is made.

— Require the offeror's key personnel to make the oral presentation.

— Schedule the oral presentations as soon as practicable after receipt of proposals.

— If award on the basis of initial proposals is not contemplated, if possible, limit the oral presentations to only those firms in the competitive range.

— Do not replicate information already requested in the written proposal in the oral presentation.

— Judiciously limit evaluation factors and subfactors to what is most important to the source selection and clearly identify the factors that apply to the oral presentation.

EFFECTIVE ORAL COMMUNICATION FOR SALES PRESENTATIONS

Effective oral communication skills can benefit people in

various fields and positions, but it cannot be taught as easily as most personal skills. Speaking effectively is extremely crucial for success in most positions in a formal working environment. It has been proven that employees spend more time speaking than writing, whether talking on the phone, conversing informally with colleagues, conducting meetings, or making sales presentations.

Research also reveals that the higher an employee moves within an organisation, the more important speaking skills become. Clearly, effective oral communication is important in all aspects of one's career. This chapter will focus only on achieving communication skills relating to sales presentations, including preparing for the presentation, making the presentation, delivery "do's and don'ts" of the presentation, and incorporating visual aids into the presentation.

Preparation

Preparation for the presentation is almost as important as the delivery of the presentation. In sales you must analyse the selling situation and the audience, determine the goal and objective of your presentation, choose and shape the content and the appropriate communication style, and organise the presentation.

Analysing the Selling Situation

When analysing the selling situation you must determine why your presentation is essential. Knowing the situation will help determine the way you shape your content and choose your style. In this analysis you need to ask yourself the following questions:

— What is the need for the presentation?

— What will happen to the organisation after the presentation?

— How does the presentation fit into the organisation's situation?

— In what surroundings will you make your presentation?

— How does your presentation relate to your audience's actions?

— How can you help the organisation?

An example of analysing the situation would be to conduct background research on the presentation audience to find out what they do, how you can benefit them, and why they asked for your presentation. Analysing the selling situation can also facilitate answers to other steps in the communication process.

Analysing the Audience

Analysing the audience can be difficult. The audience will determine the success of your presentation (your presentation is successful if your audience responds the way you intended). Effective speaking is always dependent on the audience. Identifying how your audience will respond to your presentation depends on knowing the following information about your audience: their educational and cultural background, knowledge of the subject matter, position in the organisation, and technical expertise.

Knowing your audience's personal and professional profiles will help determine what you should say, what you should not say, and the "tone" you should use. For example, you need to investigate the personalities of your audience; this will help you determine whether your style should be relaxed and informal or professional and to the point. Questions that can be used in audience analysis include the following:

— How much does my audience know about me and my presentation?
— What does the audience expect from me?
— What is the audience's attitude toward me and my product or service?
— What are the ages and gender of the audience?
— What position does the audience occupy in the organisation?
— What is the educational background of the audience?
— What are the political and religious views of the audience?
— What is the audience's personal information (outside-of-work interests)?

Determining the Goal and Objective

Determining the goal and objective of your presentation will help you design your presentation around a specific purpose. Whether you are trying to sell a product, a service, or an idea, you must keep in mind you are also selling your competence and your value to the organisation. You must make your purpose evident and relate it to your audience's perspective.

Make sure you state the main point in the beginning of the presentation so that your audience knows what the rest of the presentation will cover. State your objective in one simple sentence. For example, once you have determined your objectives, use the "T3" approach: tell them what you are going to tell them, then tell them, and finally tell them what you told them. If you use this approach you will not digress and you main points will be emphasised.

Choosing and Shaping the Content

Choosing and shaping the content can be very complicated. You want to keep your sales presentation short, interesting, and relevant. Choosing meaningful information that will appeal to your audience and situation is very important. For example, including statistics, testimonials, cases, illustrations, history, and narratives in your presentation can help convey your message. Overall, make the content interesting, but make sure it pertains to the goal of your presentation.

Choosing the Appropriate Style

Choosing the appropriate presentation style will determine the effectiveness of your content. How you speak can make or break a sales presentation. Questions you need to ask yourself as the presenter include the following:

- — What kind of tone do I want to use?
- — What kind of image do I want to create?
- — What level of language (based on audience analysis) do I use?
- — How formal should I be?
- — What approach does the audience expect from me?

The most effective style of oral communication is a conversational style because it suggests you are really talking to your audience. This type of communication includes concrete language, short sentences, and a warm and friendly tone. Do not read your presentation to the audience, this sounds impersonal and unnatural. Instead, rehearse what you are going to say because this is crucial for the success of your presentation.

Organising Your Presentation

Organising your presentation is the order in which you present your ideas. You must organise your presentation to comply with your audience's needs and perspective. Usually a presentation starts with an introduction that embodies your main point and a preview of what is ahead, the main body of information that supports the main point stated in the introduction, and a conclusion that reiterates and reinforces your main point. In the introduction grab the audience's attention, and in the conclusion leave the audience with a positive feeling about you and your product, idea, or service. MAKE AN IMPACT! For example, the opening and closing of the presentation are extremely important, so make sure you spend extra time preparing these sections. Include an interesting story or quote that relates to your presentation, it will grab the audience's attention and make your presentation memorable.

Making the Presentation

When you begin your presentation, greet your audience and create a comfortable atmosphere by starting with small talk that is unrelated to your presentation topic. After you feel prepared and comfortable, start you presentation. Stick to the plan for the presentation; tell the audience what you are going to tell them, then tell them, and at the end tell them what you have told them. Do not digress, keep to the time allowed, and when concluding ask if there are any questions. Do not leave your audience with questions; clarify all uncertainties.

"Do's and Don'ts"

Delivery entails a variety of "do's and don'ts". The following list is some of the most obvious, yet crucial do's and don'ts:

— Do speak clearly (judge the acoustics of the room);
— Don't rush or deliberately talk slow;
— Don't tell jokes;
— Don't speak in monotones (vary speed, pitch, and tone);
— Do maintain eye contact (do not look at only one individual);
— Do keep an eye on audience's body language (watch audience reactions);
— Do keep appearance clean and professional;
— Don't move around too much (i.e., pacing or nervous twitches);
— Don't talk to your visual aids;
— Do be enthusiastic and confident (it will reflect in your presentation).

Some important points to emphasise are your voice (how you say it is as important as what you say), your body language (your body movements express what your attitudes and thoughts really are), and your appearance.

The success of a sales presentation relies heavily on your delivery style. All the preparation work can go smoothly, but if you do not deliver your presentation with confidence, enjoyment, assertiveness, and enthusiasm, then all the preparation is worthless.

Visual Aids

Visual aids, if used correctly, can enhance interest in a presentation. Effective communication is both visual and verbal. According to Riceowl, visual aids can be used to show relationships among ideas so that the audience can understand and remember what you said.

The Rice on-line writing lab states that a presentation with effective visual aids is more persuasive, more professional, and more interesting than one that does not utilise visual aids. Effective visual aids should be kept simple, relate to your topic, fit the needs of the audience, and be clear and easy to understand. For example, a good visual aid would be an overhead transparency that shows a simple breakdown of numbers in pie chart form.

5

HOW TO DO A VISUAL PRESENTATION

A Presentation is a fast and potentially effective method of getting things done through other people. In managing any project, presentations are used as a formal method for bringing people together to plan, monitor and review its progress.

What can a presentation do for you?

Firstly; it puts you on display. Your staff need to see evidence of decisive planning and leadership so that they are confident in your position as their manager. They need to be motivated and inspired to undertaking the tasks which you are presenting. Project leaders from other sections need to be persuaded of the merits of your project and to provide any necessary support. Senior management should be impressed by your skill and ability so that they provide the resources so that you and your team can get the job done.

Secondly; it allows you to ask questions and to initiate discussion. It may not be suitable within the presentation formats of your company to hold a discussion during the presentation itself but it does allow you to raise the issues, present the problems and at least to establish who amongst the audience could provide valuable input to your decision-making.

Finally; presentations can be fun. They are your chance to speak your mind, to strut your stuff and to tell the people what the world is really like. While you hold the stage, the audience is bound by good manners to sit still and watch the performance.

OBJECTIVES OF COMMUNICATION

The single most important observation is that the objective of communication is not the transimission but the reception. The whole preparation, presentation and content of a speech must therefore be geared not to the speaker but to the audience. The presentation of a perfect project plan is a failure if the audience do not understand or are not persuaded of its merits. A customers' tour is a waste of time if they leave without realising the full worth of your product. The objective of communication is to make your message understood and remembered.

The main problem with this objective is, of course, the people to whom you are talking. The average human being has a very short attention span and a million other things to think about. Your job in the presentation is to reach through this mental fog and to hold the attention long enough to make your point.

The Plan

It is difficult to over estimate the importance of careful preparation. Five minutes on the floor in front of senior management could decide the acceptance of a proposal of several months duration for the manager and the whole team. With so much potentially at stake, the presenter must concentrate not only upon the facts being presented but upon the style, pace, tone and ultimately tactics which should be used. As a rule of thumb for an average presentation, no less than 1 hour should be spent in preparation for 5 minutes of talking.

Formulate your Objectives

The starting point in planning any speech is to formulate a precise objective. This should take the form of a simple, concise statement of intent. For example, the purpose of your speech may be to obtain funds, to evaluate a proposal, or to motivate your team. No two objectives will be served equally well by the same presentation; and if you are not sure at the onset what you are trying to do, it is unlikely that your plan will achieve it.

One question is: how many different objectives can you achieve, in say, 30 minutes—and the answer: not many. In the end it is far more productive to achieve one goal than to blunder over several. The best approach is to isolate the essential objective and to list at most two others which can be addressed providing they do not distract from the main one.

Focus is key. If you do not focus upon your objective, it is unlikely that the audience will.

Identify the Audience

The next task is to consider the audience to determine how best to achieve your objectives in the context of these people. Essentially this is done by identifying their aims and objectives while attending your presentation. If you can somehow convince them they are achieving those aims while at the same time achieving your own, you will find a helpful and receptive audience. For instance, if you are seeking approval for a new product plan from senior management it is useful to know and understand their main objectives. If they are currently worried that their product range is out of date and old fashioned, you would emphasise the innovative aspects of your new product; if they are fearful about product diversification you would then emphasise how well your new product fits within the existing catalogue.

This principal of matching the audience aims, however, goes beyond the simple salesmanship of an idea —it is the simplest and most effective manner of obtaining their attention at the beginning. If your opening remarks imply that you understand their problem and that you have a solution, then they will be flattered at your attention and attentive to your every word.

Structure

All speeches should have a definite structure or format; a talk without a structure is a woolly mess. If you do not order your thoughts into a structured manner, the audience will not be able to follow them. Having established the aim of your presentation you should choose the most appropriate structure to achieve it. However, the structure must not get in the way of the main message. If it is too complex, too convoluted or simply too noticeable the audience will be distracted. If a section is unnecessary to the achievement of your fundamental objectives, pluck it out.

Sequential Argument

One of the simplest structures is that of sequential argument which consists of a series of linked statements ultimately leading to a conclusion. However, this simplicity can only be achieved by careful and deliberate delineation between each section. One technique is the use of frequent reminders to the audience of the main point which have proceeded and explicit explanation of how the next topic will lead on from this.

Hierarchical Decomposition

In hierarchical decomposition the main topic is broken down into sub-topics and each sub-topics into smaller topics until eventually everything is broken down into very small basic units. In written communication this is a very powerful technique because it allows the reader to re-order the presentation at will, and to return to omitted topics at a later date. In verbal communication the audience is restricted to the order of the presenter and the hierarchy should be kept simple reinforced. As with sequential argument it is useful to summarise each section at its conclusion and to introduce each major new section with a statement of how it lies in the hierarchical order.

Question Orientated

The aim of many presentations given by managers is to either explain a previous decision or to seek approval for a plan of action. In these cases, the format can be question orientated. The format is to introduce the problem and any relevant background, and then to outline the various solutions to that problem listing the advantages and disadvantages of each solution in turn. Finally, all possible options are summarised in terms of their pro's and con's, and either the preferred solution is presented for endorsement by the audience or a discussion is initiated leading to the decision. One trick for obtaining the desired outcome is to establish during the presentation the criteria by which the various options are to be judged; this alone should allow you to obtain your desired outcome.

Pyramid

In a newspaper, the story is introduced in its entirety in a catchy first paragraph. The next few paragraphs repeat the same information only giving further details to each point. The editor then simply decides upon the newsworthiness of the report and cuts from the bottom to the appropriate number of column inches.

There are two main advantages to this style for presentations. Firstly, it can increase the audiences receptiveness to the main ideas. Since at every stage of the pyramid they have all ready become familiar with the ideas and indeed know what to expect next. This sense of *deja vu* can falsely give the impression that what they are hearing are their own ideas. The second advantage is that the duration of the talk can be easily altered by cutting the talk in exactly the same way as the newspaper editor might have done to the news story. This degree of flexibility may be useful if the same presentation is to be used several times in different situations.

Meaty sandwich

The simplest and most direct format remains the meaty sandwich. This is the simple beginning-middle-end format in which the main meat of the exposition is contained in the middle and is proceeded by an introduction and followed by a summary and conclusion. This is really the appropriate format for all small sub-sections in all the previous structures. If the talk is short enough, or the topic simple enough, it can indeed form the entirity of the presentation.

Careful Beginning

It is imperative to plan your beginning carefully; there are five main elements:

Get their attention

Too often in a speech, the first few minutes of the presentation are lost while people adjust their coats, drift in with coffee and finish the conversation they were having with the person next to them. You only have a limited time and every minute is precious to you so, from the beginning, make sure they pay attention.

Establish a theme

Basically, you need to start the audience thinking about the subject matter of your presentation. This can be done by a statement of your main objective, unless for some reason you wish to keep it hidden. They will each have some experience or opinions on this and at the beginning you must make them bring that experience into their own minds.

Present a structure

If you explain briefly at the beginning of a talk how it is to proceed, then the audience will know what to expect. This can help to establish the theme and also provide something concrete to hold their attention. Ultimately, it provides a sense of security in the promise that this speech too will end.

Create a rapport

If you can win the audience over in the first minute, you will keep them for the remainder. You should plan exactly how you wish to appear to them and use the beginning to establish that relationship. You may be presenting yourself as their friend, as an expert, perhaps even as a judge, but whatever role you choose you must establish it at the very beginning.

Administration

When planning your speech you should make a note to find out if there are any administrative details which need to be announced at the beginning of your speech. This is not simply to make yourself popular with the people organising the session but also because if these details are over looked the audience may become distracted as they wonder what is going to happen next.

The Ending

The final impression you make on the audience is the one they will remember. Thus it is worth planning your last few sentences with extreme care.

As with the beginning, it is necessary first to get their attention, which will have wandered. This requires a change of pace, a new visual aid or perhaps the introduction of one final culminating idea. In some formats the ending will be a summary of the main points of the talk.

One of the greatest mistakes is to tell the audience that this is going to be a summary because at that moment they simply switch off. Indeed it is best that the ending comes unexpectedly with that final vital phrase left hanging in the air and ringing round their memories. Alternatively the ending can be a flourish, with the pace and voice leading the audience through the final crescendo to the inevitable conclusion.

Visual Aids

Most people expect visual reinforcement for any verbal message being delivered. While it would be unfair to blame television entirely for this, it is useful to understand what the audience is accustomed to, for two reasons: firstly, you can meet their expectations using the overhead projector, a slide show, or even a video presentation; secondly, if you depart from the framework of a square picture flashed before their eyes, and use a different format, then that novelty will be most arresting. For instance, if you are describing the four functions of a project manager then display the four "hats" he/she must wear; if you are introducing the techniques of brainstorming then brandish a fishing rod to "fish for" ideas.

With traditional visual aids however, there are a few rules which should be followed to ensure they are used effectively. Most are common sense, and most are commonly ignored. As with all elements of a speech, each different viewfoil should have a distinct purpose—and if it has no purpose it should be removed. With that purpose firmly in mind you should design the viewfoil for that purpose. Some viewfoils are there to reinforce the verbal message and so to assist in recall; others are used to explain information which can be more easily displayed than discussed: and some viewfoils are designed simply for entertainment and thus to pace the presentation.

If your viewfoil is scruffy then your audience will notice that, and not what is written upon it. Do not clutter a viewfoil or it will confuse rather than assist. Do not simply photocopy information if there is more data on the page than you wish to present; in these cases, the data should be extracted before being displayed. Make sure that your writing can be read from the back of the room. Talk to the audience, not the visual aid.

Delivery

Whatever you say and whatever you show; it is you, yourself which will remain the focus of the audience's attention. If you but strut and fret your hour upon the stage and then are gone, no-one will remember what you said. The presenter has the power both to kill the message and to enhance it a hundred times beyond its worth. Your job as a manager is to use the potential of the presentation to ensure that the audience is motivated and inspired rather than disconcerted or distracted. There are five key facets of the human body which deserve attention in presentation skills: the eyes, the voice, the expression, the appearance, and how you stand.

The eyes

The eyes are said to be the key to the soul and are therefore the first and most effective weapon in convincing the audience of your honesty, openness and confidence in the objectives of your presentation. This impression may of course be totally false, but here is how to convey it.

Even when in casual conversation, your feelings of friendship and intimacy can be evaluated by the intensity and duration of eye contact. During the presentation you should use this to enhance your rapport with the audience by establishing eye contact with each and every member of the audience as often as possible. For small groups this is clearly possible but it can also be achieved in large auditoriums since the further the audience is away from the presenter the harder it is to tell precisely where he or she is looking. Thus by simply staring at a group of people at the back of a lecture theatre it is possible to convince each of them individually that he or she is the object of your attention. During presentations, try to hold your gaze fixed in specific directions for five or six seconds at a time. Shortly after each change in position, a slight smile will convince each person in that direction that you have seen and acknowledged them.

The voice

After the eyes comes the voice, and the two most important aspects of the voice for the public speaker are projection and variation. It is important to realise from the onset that few people can take their ordinary conversation voice and put it on stage. If you can, then perhaps you should move to Bollywood. The main difference comes in the degree of feedback which you can expect from the person to whom you are talking. In ordinary conversation you can see from the expression, perhaps a subtle movement of the eye, when a word or phrase has been missed or misunderstood. In front of an audience you have to make sure that this never happens. The simple advice is to slow down and to take your time.

Remember the audience is constrained by good manners not to interrupt you so there is no need to maintain a constant flow of sound. A safe style is to be slightly louder and slightly slower than a fire-side chat with slightly deaf aunt. As you get used to the sound, you can adjust it by watching the audience. A monotone speech is both boring and soporific, so it is important to try to vary the pitch and speed of your presentation. At the very least, each new sub-section should be proceeded by a pause and a change in tone to emphasise the delineation. If tonal variation does not come to you naturally try making use of rhetorical questions throughout your speech, since most British accents rise naturally at the end of a question.

Expression

The audience watch your face. If you are looking listless or distracted then they will be listless and distracted; if you are smiling, they will be wondering why and listen to find out. In normal conversation your meaning is enhanced by facial reinforcement. Thus in a speech you must compensate both for stage nerves and for the distance between yourself and the audience. The message is quite simply: make sure that your facial expressions are natural, only more so.

Appearance

There are many guides to management and presentation styles which lay heavy emphasis upon the way you dress and in the last analysis this is a matter of personal choice. That choice should however be deliberately made. When you are giving a presentation you must dress for the audience, not for yourself; if they think you look out of place, then you are. As an aside, it is my personal opinion that there exists a code of conduct among engineers which emphasises the scruffy look, and that in many organisations this tends to set the engineer apart, especially from management. It conveys the subliminal message that the engineer and the manager are not part of the same group and so hinders communication.

Stance

When an actor initially learns a new character part, he or she will instinctively adopt a distinct posture or stance to convey that character. It follows therefore that while you are on stage, your stance and posture will convey a great deal about you. The least you must do is make sure your stance does not convey boredom; at best, you can use your whole body as a dynamic tool to reinforce your rapport with the audience.

The perennial problem is what to do with your hands. These must not wave aimlessly through the air, or fiddle constantly with a pen, or (worst of all visually) juggle change in your trouser pockets. The key is to keep your hands still, except when used in unison with your speech. To train them initially, find a safe resting place which is comfortable for you, and aim to return them there when any gesture is completed.

Techniques of Speech

Every speaker has a set of "tricks of the trade" which he or she holds dear—the following are a short selection of such advice taken from various sources.

Make an impression

The average audience is very busy: they have husbands and wives, schedules and slippages, cars and mortgages; and although they will be trying very hard to concentrate on your speech, their minds will inevitably stray. Your job is to do something, anything, which captures their attention and makes a lasting impression upon them. Once you have planned your speech and honed it down to its few salient points, isolate the most important and devise some method to make it stick.

Repeat, repeat

The average audience is very busy: they have husbands or wives etc, etc—but repetition makes them hear. The average audience is easily distracted, and their attention will slip during the most important message of your speech—so repeat it. You don't necessarily have to use the resonant tonal sounds of the repeated phrase, but simply make the point again and again and again with different explanations and in different ways. The classic advice of the Sergeant Major is: "First you tell 'em what you are going to tell 'em, then you tell 'em, then you tell 'em what you told 'em!"

Draw a sign

Research into teaching has yielded the following observation: "We found that students who failed to get the point did so because they were not looking for it". If the audience knows when to listen, they will. So tell them: the important point is ... .

Draw a picture

The human brain is used to dealing with images, and this ability can be used to make the message more memorable. This means using metaphors or analogies to express your message. Thus a phrase like "we need to increase the market penetration before there will be sufficient profits for a pay related bonus" becomes "we need a bigger slice of the cake before the feast".

Jokes

The set piece joke can work very well, but it can also lead to disaster. You must choose a joke which is apt, and one which will not offend any member of the audience. This advice tends to rule out all racist, sexist or generally rude jokes. If this seems to rule out all the jokes you can think of, then you should avoid jokes in a speech.

Amusing asides are also useful in maintaining the attention of the audience, and for relieving the tension of the speech. If this comes naturally to you, then it is a useful tool for pacing your delivery to allow periods of relaxation in between your sign-posted major points.

Short and sweet

One way to polish the presentation of the main point of your speech is to consider it thus. The day before your presentation, you are called to to the office of the divisional vice-president; there you are introduced to the managing director and a representative of the company's major share holder; "O.K." says the vice president "we hear you have got something to say, we'll give you 30 seconds, *GO*". Can you do it?

If you can crystallise your thoughts and combine your main message with some memorable phrase or imagery, and present them both in 30 seconds then you have either the perfect ending or the basis for a fine presentation.

The narrative

Everyone loves a story and stories can both instruct and convey a message: Zen Philosophy is recorded in its stories, and Christianity was originally taught in parables. If you can weave your message into a story or a personal annocdote, then you can have them wanting to hear your every word—even if you have to make it up.

Rehearsal

There is no substitute for rehearsal. You can do it in front of a mirror, or to an empty theatre. In both cases, you should accentuate your gestures and vocal projection so that you get used to the sound and sight of yourself. Do not be put off by the mirror—remember: you see a lot less of yourself than your friends do.

Relaxation

If you get nervous just before the show, either concentrate on controlling your breathing or welcome the extra adrenaline. The good news is that the audience will never notice your nerves nearly as much as you think. Similarly, if you dry-up in the middle—*smile,* look at your notes, and take your time. The silence will seem long to you, but less so to the audience.

6

TIPS FOR EFFECTIVE SLIDE PRESENTATION

Slides are used in presentations for a number of different purposes. Some people use them to lull their audience to sleep, while others use them to keep their audience awake. Some use them to reveal truths, while others hide it. Some want to show what things look like, while others want to show interactions or interrelationships between things and their neighbours. Some even manage to describe the world in numbers and then turn the numbers into pictures! Your slide presentation should not, however, try to compete with rock videos or psychedelic light shows with fast paced action.

Structure your presentation so that it and its slides have a beginning, a middle and an end. Begin with a title slide followed by an overview of what your talk is about. Reinforce your major points with a summary slide at the end.

Slides for your presentation may be made in a variety of ways. These include direct colour slides which are made either in the field or research lab and black on white, white on black or white on blue slides which are usually made in the photolab from specially made artwork or from cribbed journal illustrations. The latter have copyright implications of which you should be aware. They can be direct digital images from scanners or cameras.

Artwork should generally be photographed on a copy stand with pairs of lamps mounted at a 35 degree angle or scanned on the flatbed scanner. Make sure that the ceiling lights are turned off and watch carefully for shadows on your artwork and reflections if you are using glass to hold it flat. Not all artwork can be used for all things and you may need different artwork for seminars and publication. This will particularly depend upon the amount of information and the fineness of detail in the figure.

Artwork for printed purposes can have great amounts of detailed but artwork for presentations should be kept simple and bold. In many cases it is better to use several simpler slides, each making one or two points, rather than one overly complex one. This is true in making both visually effective slides and establishing a visual rhythm in your presentation which will help keep it alive. Make sure that your lettering will be large enough to read and that lines are thick enough to show up well on the screen. The room in which you make your presentation may not darken properly and the projector may loose some of your slide's sharpness. The slides need to take this into account.

Keep extraneous stuff out of your drawings and keep them as simple as possible. Your graphs should emphasise accurate communication of information rather than imparting biases to it. Most slides and posters are created in Microsoft PowerPoint. These can be projected directly from a computer using a digital projector or they can be printed onto colour slide film with our film recorder. The film recorder is often booked up for several days and colour film is processed off campus, so leave plenty of time for your slides, ideally five days.

MAKING A SLIDE SHOW PRESENTATION

For this assignment, you will have two options:

— Create a slide presentation of a lesson that you teach and could actually use in the future. Using presentation software is an excellent way to get your point across to your students who are primarily visual learners.

— Create a slide presentation that could be running by itself in your classroom the night of Open House. This presentation would cover all of the highlights of your year.

Please note that there are many, many options in PowerPoint that won't be covered in these limited directions. What follows will only give you a jumping off point. Experimenting with the transitions, animations, and other features will only make you more comfortable with the program. Please be encouraged to do so.

Start by opening a "blank presentation" in PowerPoint. When you first open PowerPoint you will have the options of using the AutoContent wizard, a Template, or a Blank presentation. At some point you should experiment with the first two options, but for now, simply select "Blank presentation," then click on the "OK" button.

Select the "Title Slide" option. We will be coming back to this window later to select other styles of slides from the palette. Since we are just beginning, click on the option in the top left corner. You will notice that the name for that particular slide layout appears in the box in the bottom right corner. Click "OK."

Type in your title and subtitle. Simply click in the box and start typing. If you don't have a subtitle, you can leave it blank.

Select a background for the entire presentation. Under the "Format" menu select "Background." Click on the bar under the sample slide, and select "Fill Effects." Play with the Gradients, Textures, and Patterns which can be accessed by clicking on the tabs at the top of that window. Once you have selected a background you like, click on "OK." Then click the "Apply To All" button. This will put the same background on all of your slides. (Consistency is important!)

Add new slides. Under the Insert menu, select "New Slide" or click on theicon on the button bar across the top of the screen. (Getting to know these buttons can save lots of time in using any program.) Once again you see the "New Slide" palette. You may try any of these slide templates. In fact, why not take a few minutes to click on each one to see what they are. Remember that the name of each template will show up at the bottom left corner of the window. If you use any of the slides with clip art, you will be prompted to click on an area in the slide to select the clip art that you want placed there. Create all of the slides you want in your presentation before going on to the next step.

Set the transitions for your slides. You will first want to select a slide. The best way to do this is from the slide sorter view. To get there, click on the icon in the bottom left corner of the screen. This will allow you to see all of your slides at once. Click once on the first slide to select it. (Double-clicking on a slide will open that slide.) From the Slide Show menu, select "Slide Transition." On this window you may select from the many transitions that show up directly under the picture.

The words "No Transition" are part of a pop-up menu. Click on those words and slide the mouse to the transition you would like to try. A sample of that transition shows up on the sample picture. You may want to change the speed of the transitions. You can also select a sound for the transition here, but remember that sounds can be distracting if you are using this presentation to teach a lesson. If you are using this for a self-running presentation you can adjust the settings in the Advance box. (If you leave the "On mouse click" box checked, the presentation won't run by itself. When setting up a self-running presentation, be sure to leave enough time for viewers to read what is on the screens.) When you have the settings the way you want them, click on the "Apply to all" button. This will set the same transitions for all of the slides in your presentation. (You can set transitions for individual slides, but for consistency and time sake, make them the same for now.)

Add some more pizzazz to your presentation with animation! From the slide sorter view, double click on any one of your slides to see it in large view. (You cannot set custom animations from the slide sorter view, however, you can set preset animations from there.) Once in the single slide mode, select "Custom Animation" from the Slide Show menu. From this window you are given the opportunity to "bring in" each object on your slide. Several steps are necessary for this process:

— Become familiar with this window.

— Animation order shows the order that the objects will be brought into the slide.

— The picture in the top center is a preview area.

— The Timing tab lets you set the timing of each object s animation.

— The Effects tab is where you will set how you want the objects brought in and with what sound.

— The Chart Effects tab is only for slides which have charts.

— The Play Settings tab is for video clips that you have put on slides.

— Set the order for objects to be brought into the slide by clicking on the name of an object in the bottom left box, then clicking on the Animate radio dial button. (A radio dial button is a round button. When selected, it turns black in the center.) The objects will be placed in the animation order box in the top left. If the order is not correct, simply click on the name of an object and click the up or down arrows to get it into the correct order.

— Set an animation for an object by clicking on an object, then clicking on the Effects tab. Under "Entry animation and sound" click on the top pop-up menu to see a list of all of the animations available. Select one from the list. Then select a sound from the next pop-up menu. For a text object, you have options on the right for introducing text. You may want to take time to experiment with those.

— Before clicking OK, click on the Preview button to see if everything is set the way you want it. If not, change it now. If you like it, click on OK.

Run your slide show! It is always good practice to run through your presentation several times to make sure that things are how you want them. If you don't like something, change it. To run the show, get to the first slide, either by clicking on it in the slide sorter view, or by scrolling up to it using the scroll bar. Then, click on the icon at the bottom left of the screen. To stop the presentation in the middle, press the escape "esc" key on the keyboard.

TIPS FOR EFFECTIVE SLIDE PRESENTATIONS

Fill space on the slide effectively: Bring the top, bottom, left, and right edges of your image near to the respective borders of the slide.

Choose font sizes carefully: People in the back of the lecture/seminar room should be able to read the text; when in doubt, use a bigger font.

Beware of the "portrait" orientation: Many times the bottom of a "portrait" slide will be projected below eye-level; if you must use these, be sure that you preview them to adjust the size and height to maximise visibility.

Avoid "mega data" slides: If you put too much on a slide, you will lose your audience no matter how good a job you do explaining the contents; "mega data" slides also tend to include small font sizes making it difficult for audiences to read.

Use no more than two graphs on a slide: This is a specific case of #4, above; if you must use more than two graphs, make the lessons in each simple and obvious.

Use colors that contrast: Colour choice is a key feature to the effective communication process. Optimal colour choices should complement the physiology of human vision and perception rather than just being your own "favourites". It is best to stick with contrasting combinations of Red, Green, Blue, Yellow, Black, and White whenever possible; but, beware of certain combinations like red letters on a blue background (causes "stereopsis") or red/green combinations (many people are red/green colourblind). When in doubt, ask for the opinions of a few friends/colleagues.

Ideas for emphasis: The best way to provide emphasis of ideas, points, bullets, words, phrases, paragraphs, and the like is with bold fonts, *italic* fonts, or different colors. A surprisingly ineffective way to emphasise is with underlining.

Multicolour/ gradient backgrounds: These look very nice, but can cause perceptibility problems when text and graphics contain colours that contrast with part, but not all, of the gradient. Again, choose colours carefully, and ask for an opinion if you are in doubt. Finally, vertical gradients are generally better than horizontal gradients.

Slide contents should be self evident: Give the slide a title, label all graph axes, lines, bars, and insets. Use colours to help discriminate key portions of complex schemes. But, even though your slides are self evident, be sure to explain what the slide shows and how it shows it. Also, avoid the presence of data that you are not going to talk about; remake the slides if necessary!

Avoid simply reading the slide to the audience: Though your slides may be self-evident, you can best keep the interest of most audiences by explaining the content using related wording to what is depicted; variety is the spice of life!

Use laser pointers sparingly: Highlight only what your talk is focused on and be sure to move the pointer slowly. Once you have drawn the attention to the given point, turn the pointer off. Not only will this remove distraction, but it will also conserve the (rapidly draining) batteries in the laser pointer. It also helps to say things like, "as you see in the lower panel of the slide..." when you use the laser pointer.

Avoid "laser light shows": This is a point added in emphasis of #10 above. Have you ever noticed seminar speakers who wave the laser pointer wildly all over their slide, the walls, ceilings, etc.? Need we say more?!

Prepare your slides well in advance: What you envisioned during slide creation may not be what is actually seen upon projection! Computers and/or cameras don't always accurately map/record colours.

WYSIWYG can be WYSINWYG! A little extra time will allow you to edit your slides and reshoot them.

Allow no more than 1-2 slides per minute of presentation: More usually causes you to rush through your presentation, thereby increasing the chance of losing your audience or skipping pertinent information. When in doubt, use fewer slides. A little "extra" time at the end of a talk may allow/spark lively discussion.

Speak comfortably and clearly: In fact, it is even a good idea to speak a bit more slowly than your normal pace. This really helps the comprehension of your listeners! A corrolary is "Never rush!".

Enjoy your presentation: Remember "infectious laughter"? A good attitude will rub off on your listeners and they will enjoy the talk more as well.

Use dark background with light text. (Although note that if you are presenting in a bright room, it may be easier to see a slide with a light background. Thanks to Lorrie Cranor for pointing this out to me.)

Use sans serif font such as Arial or Helvetica. (For example, do not use Times, it's harder to read in a distance.)

Use large font, never as little as 12 point.

When displaying data (findings via numbers or quotes) consider using a different font, e.g. Courier bold, for emphasis. And although Courier is not sans-serif, it is big and bulky and can be read from afar.

If you can barely fit it on the slide then it's too much material. Unless everyone in the room can see all the details, get rid of some of the information. You don't want people to be distracted by squiting and trying to guess what's on your slides.

Minimise distractions. Do not display too many graphics and be very selective with the use of animations.

Remember the importance of white space, or perhaps we should just call it "blank space". Leaving some space on the slide blank is very important to making it an accessible slide.

If you have a lot to say, consider writing bullet point words instead of sentences or split up the slide's content into two slides.

7

CREATING EFFECTIVE POWERPOINT PRESENTATION

MAKING POWERPOINT PRESENTATIONS

— Selecting Templates in PowerPoint

— To attach a template to an existing presentation

— Open a new or existing PowerPoint presentation.

From the Format menu, select Apply Design Template. The Presentation Designs folder appears in the Apply Design dialog. The folder contains design templates. Design templates contain pre-designed formats and colour schemes to give presentations a custom and professional look.

Choose a presentation template and click Apply.

Creating Unique PowerPoint Design Templates

A template is a foundation from which you create a presentation. A template can provide backgrounds for slides, font selection, text placeholders, and other design elements. A template can also provide a foundation for presentation content. PowerPoint comes with two types of templates. The most common template is a design template; the other is a content template. A design template contains pre-designed formats and colour schemes. These features help to give a presentation a custom look.

Using one of the existing PowerPoint templates, you can create your own PowerPoint design template quite easily.

To create a unique PowerPoint design template

Access the presentation that will serve as the foundation for your work. You have two options from which to choose:

— Open an existing PowerPoint presentation, or

— Open one of the PowerPoint design templates. Open PowerPoint. Select Open from the File menu. Under Files of type, select Presentation Templates (*.pot). Navigate to the appropriate folder, usually c:/Program Files/Microsoft Office/Templates/ Presentation Designs. Click Open.

Change the template to suit your needs. You can change the colour scheme, default font, etc. Make sure that you use the Slide Master to change the background items or the appearance of the font.

On the File menu, click Save As.

Enter a name for the design template, and then click Design Template in the Save as type box.

Choose a location in which to save the template. You can save your design template in one of your own folders, or you can save it with the other design templates in the Presentation Designs folder. If you want to be able to easily select this template to attach to future presentations, store it in the Presentation Designs folder, Program Files/Microsoft Office/Templates/Presentation Designs.

Click Save.

PowerPoint" border=0 height=40 src="/images/title_tutorials_powerpoint2.gif" width=585

Creating Unique PowerPoint Content Templates

A template is a foundation from which you create a presentation. A template can provide backgrounds for slides, font selection, text placeholders, and other design elements. A template can also provide a foundation for presentation content. PowerPoint comes with two types of templates. The most common template is a design template; the other is a content template. Content templates contain formats and colour schemes just like design templates, plus suggested content for specific subjects. For example, existing PowerPoint content templates provide structure for company meetings, personal introductions, and team motivation.

To create a unique PowerPoint content template,

Access the presentation that will serve as the foundation for your work. You have two options from which to choose:

- Open an existing PowerPoint presentation. Choose one that has the basic content from which you want to work, or
- Open one of the PowerPoint content templates. Open PowerPoint. Select Open from the File menu. Under Files of type, select Presentation Templates (*.pot). Navigate to the appropriate folder, usually c:/Program Files/Microsoft Office/Templates/Presentations. Click Open.

Change the template to suit your needs. You can change subject matter, details, organisation, etc. Make sure that you use the Slide Master to change background items or the appearance of the font.

On the File menu, click Save As.

Enter a name for the content template, and then click Content Template in the Save as type box.

Choose a location in which to save the template. You can save your content template in one of your own folders, or you can save it with the other content templates in the Presentations folder. If you want to be able to easily select this template to attach to future presentations, store it in the Presentations folder, Program Files/Microsoft Office/Templates/Presentations.

Click Save.

Working with PowerPoint Colour Schemes

PowerPoint comes with pre-installed colour schemes. These schemes contain eight complementary colours. Specific colours are assigned to headline, body, background, etc. You can assign a colour scheme to the following: a "blank" presentation, a presentation based on a presentation design template, and on a presentation based on a presentation (content) template. So, when you choose a template for your presentation, don't worry too much about the default colour choice. You can always change that later.

To choose a colour scheme,

Open an existing PowerPoint presentation or create a new one. Remember, you can attach a colour scheme to any presentation, so feel free to use whatever template you desire or start from scratch.

On the Format menu, select Slide Colour Scheme.

On the Standard tab, select the desired colour scheme and click Apply to All.

What if you want to change a colour later?

If you use only the colours supplied in the colour scheme (the default colours that appear whenever you are given the option to select colour), and you later want to change the colour scheme: No problem. PowerPoint replaces the original colours with ones from the new scheme. However, if you select a colour scheme and then make an arbitrary change, Power Point does not replace the aberrant colour if you choose a new colour scheme.

Background colour

What are the best colours to use as backgrounds? In general, cool colours make better backgrounds. These colours include shades of blue and green. Additionally, purple may work well as a background. Conversely, the worst backgrounds are usually the "hot" colours. These include red and orange. However, both of these colours make excellent choices for graphics such as charts and diagrams. Yellow also does not work well as a background.

There are, of course, exceptions to the rule. One of the best presentations that we have ever seen used a red and maroon striped background.

Changing background graphics

Most PowerPoint presentations make use of templates that contain colour schemes, formatted text, and often graphics. These templates help to give slide presentations a consistent appearance. Instead of having to determine a background colour for every slide, you can simply select a template that contains the desired background colour.

While templates provide convenience and consistency, there are times when you need to modify a particular slide within a presentation. You may want to remove a background graphic from one slide without changing the background for all of the other slides. So, instead of making the change on the Master slide, you need to make it on the individual slide.

To change the background graphic in PowerPoint

Open a PowerPoint presentation,

Navigate to the desired slide or create a new one.

First you must omit the background graphic:

— Select Background from the Format menu.

— Select Omit background graphics from master.

— Click Apply.

Then, you add the new graphic to the slide:

— From the Insert menu, select Picture > Clip Art or From File.

— Navigate to the desired graphic. Click Insert.

Using a Full Screen Picture as a Background

Some presentations benefit from using a photograph or single graphic as a background image. There are many ways to do this in PowerPoint, but the easiest way is listed here.

To use a full screen picture as a background

Open a PowerPoint presentation.

On the View menu, select Master > Slide Master.

On the Format menu, select Background.

Click the down arrow on the colour bar.

Select Fill Effects > Picture > Select Picture.

Locate the image you want to choose and click OK.

Click OK again.

Click Apply to All.

PowerPoint automatically scales the image to fit the screen. This is a wonderful way to integrate a graphic element into a presentation. However, because PowerPoint automatically sizes the graphic, the clarity of the graphic is impacted by its original size. So, a graphic that is originally 1" x 1" may become unrecognisable as PowerPoint resizes it. Consequently, it is best to use images that are relatively close in size to the final slide size.

Inserting Vertical Slides in Horizontal PowerPoint Presentations

Most Microsoft PowerPoint presentations use a landscape orientation. (The presentation slides are wider than they are tall). This layout is usually more desirable for reading text and charts. Consider the outdoor billboard, for example. However, there may be times when you want to create a presentation using a portrait layout (slides are taller than they are wide). Though unusual, this is possible with PowerPoint.

To create a PowerPoint presentation with vertical slides

Open a new existing PowerPoint presentation.

Click File > Page Setup.

Under Orientation, Slides, choose Portrait.

Click OK.

All slides will be laid out vertically.

Are there ever instances in which you would want to use both types of slide layouts in the same presentation? Perhaps. Consider a presentation that uses a "traditional" horizontal slide layout. It is full of text and the occasional graphic.

Insert vertical slides within a horizontal slide presentation

If you want a traditional, horizontal presentation to include vertical slides (with the portrait orientation), you must create two presentations: one for the horizontal slides and one for the vertical slide(s) . . .

— Create the horizontal PowerPoint presentation.

— Create the vertical PowerPoint presentation.

Store these two presentations in the same folder.

Open the horizontal presentation (this is the main presentation) and go to the slide from which you want to jump to the vertical presentation.

Select the text or graphic to use as a hyperlink.

Click Insert > Hyperlink.

Select the name of the vertical presentation. Then click OK.

Save and run the horizontal presentation to test.

Cropping Graphics in PowerPoint

Cropping is a familiar photographic term that means cutting off an unwanted part of a picture. Cropping is also used when referring to graphic images. Microsoft PowerPoint allows you to crop images as desired using a simple dragging motion. This is an especially useful feature when you are working with existing graphics in a new or edited presentation. While you may want to use many of the existing graphic images, you may not need them in their entirety. Of course you could simply modify the existing graphics and reinsert them in the presentation. But what can you do when the original graphics are embedded (not linked) — and you don't have the source files? Fortunately, you can skip recreating the graphics and just crop them as desired.

To crop a graphic in PowerPoint

Open the desired PowerPoint presentation and navigate to the slide that contains the graphic to edit.

Enable the Picture toolbar. (On the View menu, select Toolbars > Picture).

Select the graphic to crop. After selecting a graphic, all tools on the Picture toolbar should appear "active" — not grayed out.

Click the Crop tool. This is the selected tool above. (Roll over tools and hold for a tool description to appear).

Position the Crop tool on one of the handles around the selected graphic — in the area you wish to crop. Slowly drag toward the center of the graphic. The dotted line shows what is cropped.

When you are finished, release the mouse button. The cropped graphic appears on the slide. If you make a mistake, simply select CTRL + Z to undo the crop.

Inserting Digital Images

Digital images come from a variety of sources. You can create digital images yourself using a digital camera, or you can use images that are already created.

To insert a digital image in a presentation

Open a PowerPoint presentation.

Navigate to the slide in which you want to add the image.

On the Insert menu, select Picture > From File.

Select the desired image and click Insert

Using the mouse, place the image where you want it to appear.

Optional: If you want to edit the image (crop, recolour, add a border, etc.), select the image and right-click. Select Format Picture. The following dialog appears.

Make changes as desired and click OK.

Creating Transparent Graphics

At times, you may want to insert a "transparent" graphic into a PowerPoint presentation. This means the background colour of the graphic "disappears", and the central image lies on the slide background. For example, assume you are working with a presentation that has a dark green background. You want to insert a graphic of a woman. You inherited this particular graphic; you did not create it. When you insert this graphic in your presentation, the white background of the file makes the presentation look amateurish. Instead, you would like the central image (the woman) to appear simply on top of the green slide background. Fortunately, this is easy to accomplish.

Before you begin

You should know two things about transparent graphics:

— You can make only one colour transparent.

— This option is not available for all clip art.

To create a transparent graphic,

Open a PowerPoint presentation.

If necessary, insert the desired picture.

Select the picture you wish to make transparent.

On the Picture toolbar, click Set Transparent Colour. The cursor changes.

Click the colour (in the graphic) you want to make transparent. PowerPoint replaces all instances of this colour with the background colour.

Inserting Digital Photos

Digital cameras have made it extraordinarily simple to include photographs in presentations, in no time! You don't have to worry about developing film or hard copies. Just click and go.

To insert a digital photo in a presentation

Using a digital camera, take the desired photo.

Download the photo to your computer.

Open a PowerPoint presentation.

Navigate to the slide in which you want to add the photo.

On the Insert menu, select Picture and click the down arrows.

Select From Scanner or Camera.

Select the desired photo and click Insert.

Using the mouse, place the photo where you want it to appear.

Optional: If you want to edit the photo (crop, recolour, add a border, etc.), select the photo and right-click. Select Format Picture. The following dialog appears.

Make changes as desired and click OK.

Inserting Scanned Photos

Add some zing to your next presentation by inserting a scanned photo! It's quick, easy, and takes your presentation to a new level. Follow the step-by-step instructions below.

To insert a scanned photo in a presentation

Scan the desired photo.

Open a PowerPoint presentation.

Navigate to the slide in which you want to add the photo.

On the Insert menu, select Picture and click the down arrows.

Select From Scanner or Camera.

Edit the photo as desired.

The image appears in Microsoft Photo Editor, an application that provides editing capabilities. If you select Typical setup when you installed PowerPoint, you have already installed Photo Editor. To verify that Photo Editor is installed, make sure that you are in Slide view. From the Insert menu, select Object. The following dialog box appears. Note that you can insert many types of objects.

Inserting Clip Art

To insert clip art in PowerPoint presentations.

Open a PowerPoint presentation.

Navigate to the desired slide or create a new one.

From the Insert menu, select one of the following:

— Picture > Clip Art

— Use this option if you want to insert a vector image such as an .eps, .wmf, and .drw file.

— The Microsoft Clip Gallery appears. Navigate to the desired graphic. Click Insert. Note that you can also select Clip Properties to check out file name, type, size, and path. You can also select Import Clips to add clip art to the Clip Gallery.

— Picture > From File

— Use this option if you want to insert a Raster image such as a bitmap, a digital photo, or a scanned image. Usually these files have one of the following extensions: .bmp, .tif, .gif, .jpg, or .pcx.

— Navigate to the desired graphic. Click **Insert**.

Inserting Drawing Objects Multiple Times

Have you ever wanted to insert the same drawing object several times on a PowerPoint slide? Take a look at this slide, for example:

This is a slide from a literature presentation that covers Albert Camus's "The Stranger". The teacher who wrote this presentation wanted to cover the topic of imagery — and specifically, he wanted to discuss the way the heat of the sun continually beats upon the protagonist in the work. So, he decided to create a simple slide (black background) and a slightly abstract sun graphic (the orange ellipse) with the Oval Drawing tool in PowerPoint. Then, he decided to copy this object several times on the edge of the slide — offering the impression of a weight hovering nearby.

Of course, the teacher could have created the sun object one time. Then, he could have selected the object and performed a sequence of "copy/paste" actions again and again to replicate the sun six times. However, this teacher could also have replicated the drawing object a bit easier — with a little-known PowerPoint feature: the "sticky" feature. PowerPoint allows you to make the Drawing tool "sticky" so you can add an object with a simple mouse-click. It is easy to do!

To insert a drawing object multiple times,

Open the desired PowerPoint presentation and navigate to the desired slide.

Make sure the Drawing toolbar is visible. (Right-click any toolbar and select Drawing.) Notice the Drawing Rectangle — it is highlighted when it is "sticky".

To insert a drawing object several times, double-click the chosen drawing object button (such as the Rectangle or the Oval) on the Drawing toolbar. The button stays selected or "sticky."

Insert your drawing object several times by clicking wherever you want the object to appear.

When you're finished inserting the objects, click the drawing object button again, or press ESC.

Adding Animated GIFs

Animated GIFs are everywhere on the web. In fact, this is the most popular type of animation. But what is an animated GIF?

A GIF (Graphics Interchange Format) is a bitmapped file format that supports colour and various resolutions and also includes data compression. An animated GIF combines several images into a single GIF file. While it doesn't provide the same level of control and flexibility as other animation formats, GIF animation is extremely popular because it is supported by nearly all web browsers. In addition, animated GIF files tend to be smaller than many other animation file types — such as Java applets.

How Does PowerPoint Deal with Animated GIFs?

You can add animated GIFs to PowerPoint presentations as you would nearly any other graphic. This type of file does have certain idiosyncratic behaviors, however. While you are working on a PowerPoint presentation, animated GIFs appear static. During a slide show, animated GIFs play automatically.

To insert an animated GIF

Open the desired PowerPoint presentation and navigate to the slide to which you want to add the GIF.

Select Insert > Picture > Clip Art.

Select the Motion Clips tab.

Select the desired Category. Then, select the desired GIF and Insert Clip.

— If you want to insert a GIF not found in the Microsoft Clip Art Gallery, click **Import Clips**.

— If you want to search the Microsoft web site for FREE animated GIFs, click **Clips Online**.

When you are finished adding the GIF to the slide, click Close (X).

Drawing Perfectly Straight Lines

If you have ever used the line drawing tool in PowerPoint, you know it can be tricky to get the lines perfectly straight. This is especially true if you are using the pointer tool from a laptop or while you are presenting. And even those lines that look straight when you are creating them can often appear jagged when projected . . .

The white line shown here looks nearly straight in the Slide View of the presentation. Yet, it is only when projected that you see it is not perfectly straight . . .

Fortunately, there is an easy way to guarantee straight lines in PowerPoint.

To draw a perfectly straight line

Open the PowerPoint presentation and navigate to the slide in which you want to draw the line.

Click on the Line Drawing Tool.

Draw the line as you would normally — however, hold down the Shift key as you do so.

Making Fonts Look the Same in Electronic and Printed PowerPoint Presentations

When working with PowerPoint (especially when using older versions of PowerPoint and Windows), there may be times when you notice a disparity between the way a font looks in an electronic presentation and the way it appears when printed. Consider the following example:

Slide A—This slide comes from the original electronic presentation.

Slide B—This is how the slide appears when printed. Notice the difference in font.

Slide A (from the electronic presentation) appears as the creator intended. Notice the stylised font. However, when this same slide is printed (Slide B), notice the font substitution. (In this case the font is switched to the standard Arial.) Specifically, the printer is substituting one font for another — the known, generic Arial for the unknown.

Of course, this font substitution may not present a problem. If the electronic presentation is the only thing the audience sees, perhaps there is no difficulty with a font substitution. However, if the fonts used in the slides are part of a greater look and feel, much may be lost with a substitution. Additionally, the layout of text may vary greatly from one font usage to another. Notice in the example above how much smaller the Arial text (Slide B) appears. What would happen if it were larger than the original . . . In that case, all of the text may not even appear on the printed slide.

So, how to correct this problem? Fortunately the answer is simple. Just use a TrueType font — and both electronic and printed slides will appear the same!

To use a TrueType font

Open the desired PowerPoint presentation.

Add and select text as desired.

Select Format > Font.

In the Font field, choose any font with the TrueType symbol. Notice the TT designation. This denotes a TrueType font. Also, notice the reminder at the bottom of the dialog box.

Click OK.

Importing Text from Other Applications into PowerPoint

When you need to create an electronic presentation, you don't always start from scratch. Frequently you may have existing documentation of some sort, and rather than meticulously "cutting and pasting" (or even worse, re-typing the text), you simply import your existing information directly into PowerPoint. You can use text created in other programs to make a new presentation or add slides to an existing presentation.

PowerPoint imports documentation in outline format. (For an example of outline format in Microsoft Word, open a Word document, select Outline from the View menu.) PowerPoint uses the outline structure from the styles in the original document to create logical slide order and content. Therefore, text order is consistent with the original file. Text styles in the original document determine slide text: a Heading 1 becomes a slide title, a Heading 2 style becomes the first level of text, and so on.

If the document contains no styles, PowerPoint uses the existing paragraph indentations to create the outline.

To convert a Word document into a PowerPoint file

You can easily create a presentation from an existing Word document.

Open the document in Microsoft Word.

From the File menu, select the down arrows and then select Send To > Microsoft PowerPoint.

Each paragraph formatted with the Heading 1 style becomes the title of a new slide, each paragraph formatted with the Heading 2 style becomes the first level of text, and so on.

To convert a non-Word document into a PowerPoint file

When you import outlines from other word processing programs, PowerPoint reads the documents in rich-text format (.rtf) and plain text format. All first-level headings in an imported outline become slide titles, and body text becomes indent levels. The slide master in the current presentation determines the format for the title and text.

Embossing Text in PowerPoint

Embossing text means giving it a raised effect. It should look as though the text has been stamped onto the "page" from the reverse side. This is a highly artistic way of using fonts and must be used sparingly if you plan to project your presentation. Embossing is best used in moderation.

To emboss text:

Open a PowerPoint presentation.

Add text as desired.

Highlight text.

From the Format menu, select Font.

Select Emboss and click OK.

Turning Off Automatic Hyperlinks in Pasted Text (Word)

Have you ever pasted a chunk of text from a web page directly into a Microsoft Word document? If so, you may have noticed the entire block of text act as a hyperlink. What if you want to delete part of the text and make other changes — unfortunately, you can't. The text behaves as if it were a large graphic — and in essence, it is. It is a hyperlink block — and if you try to edit it, you "activate" the link — your browser launches with the linked page in view.

To turn off automatic hyperlinks on "pasted" text

Open Word and create the document as desired.

Copy and paste the selection that contains the hyperlink. (You may not even know a text block is hyperlinked until you go to edit it.)

Move the mouse over the hyperlink section of text. (The mouse should change into a pointing hand.)

Right-click.

Select Hyperlink > Edit Hyperlink.

Click Remove Link. The hyperlink is removed and you can edit the text as desired.

Shadowing Text in PowerPoint

Shadows can add a professional look to text. There are two quick and easy ways to add shadow to texts in PowerPoint.

To add default shadow to text

Open a PowerPoint presentation.

Add text as desired.

Highlight the text.

Select Format > Font.

Select Shadow and click OK

To customize shadow on text

Open a PowerPoint presentation.

Add text as desired.

Highlight text and click the Shadow (insert button image) button from the PowerPoint Drawing toolbar.

Do one of the following:

— Choose a shadow angle. PowerPoint automatically shadows text, or

— Click Shadow Settings. The following dialog appears.

— You can make adjustments to the shadow in this dialog. If you want to make further adjustments, such as choosing the shadow colour, click the down arrow.

— Choose settings as desired.

Adding Narration

You can add narration to PowerPoint presentations provided you have a sound card and a microphone. You can record narration for the presentation, or you can record narration during a presentation, thereby including audience comments.

Narration takes precedence over all sounds within a presentation. So, you should not include sound files in a presentation that includes narration, as those sound files would not be played.

To record narration

Open a PowerPoint presentation.

On the Slide Show menu, click Record Narration. A dialog box appears showing the amount of free disk space and the number of minutes you can record.

Do one of the following:

— To insert the narration as an embedded object, click OK.

— To insert the narration as a linked object, select the Link narrations in checkbox. Browse to the desired folder if necessary. Then, click OK to begin recording.

PowerPoint switches to Slide Show. Record narration as desired.

When the Slide Show is finished, a message appears:

— To save the timings along with the narration, click Yes.

— To save only the narration, click No.

You know which slides contain narration because those slides contain a sound icon in the lower right corner.

Inserting Sound in PowerPoint Presentations

To insert sound in a PowerPoint presentation

Open a PowerPoint Presentation.

Navigate to the desired slide or create a new one.

From the Insert menu, select one of the following:

— *Movies and Sound > Sound from Gallery:* The Microsoft Clip Gallery appears. Navigate to the desired sound file. Click Insert. If you want to test the sound file, click Play. Note that you can also select Clip Properties to check out file name, type, size, and path. You can also select Import Clips to add a sound file to the Clip Gallery.

— *Movies and Sound > From File:* Use this option to insert a sound file that is not located in the Clip

Gallery. Navigate to the desired graphic. Click Insert.

The PowerPoint speaker icon appears on the slide. Move it to the desired location.

PowerPoint" border=0 height=40 src="/images/title_tutorials_powerpoint2.gif" width=585

Inserting Sound Buttons in PowerPoint Presentations

PowerPoint makes it easy to do all sorts of things through the use of action buttons. You simply add an action button to a presentation. Then, you define how to use this button during the slide show. Consider the following options:

— Jump from one presentation to another without closing the first one

— Jump to a slide not contained in order

— Insert a sound

— Go to an Internet address

Creating Tables

You can use many standard Microsoft Office programs to create a table: Microsoft Word, Microsoft Excel, or Microsoft Access. Then, you can insert the table in a PowerPoint presentation.

To insert a Word table in PowerPoint

Open a PowerPoint presentation in Slide view.

From the Insert menu, select Picture > Microsoft Word Table. The Insert Word Table dialog appears.

Select the desired number of rows and columns; then click OK. Power creates a placeholder for you in which to work.

Create the table as desired. Enter the data in the table cells. Use the Word tools and menus to format the table. For example, to add borders to the table, use the AutoFormat command on the Table menu.

Then, click outside the table. PowerPoint inserts the table in the slide. If you want to edit the table, simply double-click on the table.

Rotating Charts

Rotating most slide objects in PowerPoint is an easy thing to do. You simply select the object to rotate — then, click the Free Rotate tool and choose the degree of rotation.

Rotating charts, however, is a bit more complex than rotating other objects. When you select a chart, the rotate tools are dimmed and therefore unavailable. Nevertheless, you can rotate a chart in PowerPoint by rotating the plot area to change the angle from which you view the plotted series.

To rotate a chart in PowerPoint:

Open the PowerPoint presentation that contains the chart to rotate and navigate to the correct slide.

Double-click on the chart you want to rotate.

From the PowerPoint main menu, select Chart > 3-D View. The 3-D View dialog appears. This dialog allows you to change many aspects of the chart view.

If you wanted the chart to rotate so that the 4th quarter results were listed first — on the left — you would enter 180 in the Rotation box. This would rotate the chart 180 degrees.

Inserting Organisation Charts

There are several ways of adding organisation charts to PowerPoint presentations. You can create a chart or table in a variety of applications and then copy or link the file to a PowerPoint presentation.

Microsoft Organisation Chart allows you to create a new chart using one of two templates. The templates contain boxes with fields/labels. You can edit labels and add boxes as desired. Then, you can embed the chart in or link the chart to a PowerPoint presentation. When you embed an object, you place a copy of the original object in the client document. It is then completely separate from the original chart. You can edit the embedded object independently from the original. When you link an object to a client document, the object appears in the client document, but it still resides in the original document. The client document is automatically updated when you make a change to the object in the original document.

Setting Slide Transitions and Timing

Most electronic presentation applications allow you to set animated transitions between slides. You can set slide transitions to fade out, dissolve, roll from the left, etc. These transitions provide a smooth change from one slide to another — whether you are manually clicking through slides or automatically advancing through slides. Additionally, most applications, including PowerPoint, also allow you to set a specific time (duration) for each slide. This means you can determine how long a slide is visible before advancing to the next slide when running a presentation automatically. This type of custom timing for slides is necessary whenever you create a presentation to advance automatically. It is not difficult to do — but it can be time-consuming to implement because timing the slides correctly takes several tries.

To set slide transitions and timing in PowerPoint

Create the content for the PowerPoint presentation.

Edit the presentation to the point at which you feel comfortable with the content. When you are satisfied with the content, graphics, and overall design of the presentation, you are ready to determine the slide transitions.

Timing Automatic PowerPoint Presentations

PowerPoint presentations can be designed to advance manually — with the help of a presenter — or automatically — in which slides advance on automatic cues — by preset timing. Automatic presentations are not simply used for trade shows or self-running kiosks. They are also ideal for use whenever you want to have a "hands-free" presentation and feel comfortable that the presentation will not need to be interrupted. For example, an automatic presentation might work well if you wanted to create a highly theatrical presentation (usually relatively brief), in which you moved around to interact with props. In this case, you could create an automatic presentation in which slides advance on predetermined times.

In any case, there are two ways to set slide timing in automatic presentations:

— through the Slide Transition dialog, or

— through the Rehearsal dialog.

Using the Slide Transition dialog

The Slide Transition dialog allows you to set slide transitions and timing. You can assign a slide transition to a particular slide and also determine how many seconds lapse before the next slide appears. This is a precise way of determining slide timing to be sure. However, it is a hit and miss approach that often requires many rounds of testing. For example, you may set a slide's transition timing to 20 seconds, only to find when testing that this is way too long. Then, you return to the Slide Transition dialog to correct the problem — and change the timing to 8 seconds. You test it again — and find this is not enough time. Finally, after many rounds of testing, you find 13 seconds is ideal for a particular slide. GREAT. What if the presentation has 30 slides? Isn't there a better way of setting slide timing?

Yes, there is a much better way of setting slide timing. You can use a little known PowerPoint tool called the Rehearsal dialog.

Using the Rehearsal dialog

Instead of using the Slide Transition (or Custom Animation) dialogs to set slide timing, you can set slide timing while you rehearse a slide show.

To time automatic PowerPoint presentations using the Rehearsal dialog

Create the content for the PowerPoint presentation.

Edit the presentation to the point at which you feel comfortable with the content.

When you are satisfied with the content, graphics, and overall design of the presentation, you are ready to determine the slide transitions and timing. Set the slide transitions.

Select Slide Show > Rehearse Timings. The slideshow starts, and the Rehearsal dialog is displayed.

Advance through each animation on the slide at the speed you feel is appropriate.

Advance through each slide at the speed you feel is appropriate.

When you are done with the presentation, a confirmation dialog appears — asking if you want to save the recorded times. Click Yes to save the times.

Assuming the presentation is automatic (designed to run without mouse clicks by the presenter), confirm this selection. Select Slide Show > Set Up Show.

Under Advance slides, make sure Using timings, if present is selected. Click OK.

During the slideshow, the presentation slides will advance at the time specified during the Rehearsal.

Creating Individual Slide Shows

Have you ever needed to create a presentation for several audiences — making minor changes to the presentation for each audience? For example, maybe you need to create a comprehensive product development presentation to deliver to the financial folks, the marketing team, and a co-development group. Essentially the core presentation is the same for all audiences. However, you want to keep several slides pertaining to finances away from the co-development group. You also don't want to share all of the marketing challenges with the financial group. What can you do?

You can create a single comprehensive presentation, save it as several file names, open each presentation and make the changes you need, and resave the individual presentations. Then you can keep track of all these presentations! Is there another way? Yes, there is . . .

PowerPoint allows you to adapt a single presentation to a variety of audiences by creating "custom shows" within the presentation. This saves you the effort of duplicating a whole presentation, saving it as a new file, and modifying it to suit a new audience.

Custom shows are shows within a presentation, created from slides that you group together. You can group slides into as many different custom shows as you like. You name each custom show, and when you deliver the presentation, you just select the desired custom show.

To create a custom show in PowerPoint

Custom shows are contained within one presentation file, but they run independently of each other.

Open PowerPoint and create the comprehensive presentation. (This presentation should include all of the slides you want to possibly show)

Select Slide Show > Custom Shows. Then click New. The Define Custom Show dialog box appears.

In the Slides in presentation box., select the slides you want to include in the custom show. Click Add.

You can change the order of the slides as you like. To change the order in which the slides appear in the show, select a slide in the Slides in custom show list, then click the Up or Down arrow as desired.

In the Slide show name box, enter a name for the custom show.

Click OK. The Custom Shows dialog returns.

Click Show to preview the custom show. Click through the slides. You should see only the slides for the custom show.

Exit the slide show to return to the default PowerPoint view.

Creating Simple Menus for PowerPoint Presentations

We all know the power of the menu. We see standard menus in the applications we use every day; we see complex menus as we use OLE applications, and we use menus to navigate web sites.

Menus allow us to navigate, and they allow us to select options. However, they also serve a subliminal role as well. A menu can serve as a visual foundation, even when we do not "use" the menu for specific purposes. For example, you may be a power user of Microsoft Word who uses shortcuts rather than menus to access features. Nevertheless, the simple sight of the menu provides a visual grounding within the application.

Menus can also provide a foundation or sense of organisation within an electronic presentation. These menus can be static and simply serve an aesthetic function. They can also be interactive. You can place action buttons on "menu items" to give an electronic presentation a "web" feel.

Creating Agenda Slides in PowerPoint

There are two ways to create an agenda slide (or an overview slide) in PowerPoint. The first way to create an agenda slide makes a simple slide, complete with all selected items. The second way to create an agenda slide creates more than just a list of items to be covered. It is actually an interactive slide that allows you to jump from the agenda slide to a supporting slide then jump back to the agenda slide, and so on . . .

To create a quick agenda slide

Create a PowerPoint presentation as you like. Do not create the agenda or overview slide.

In Slide Sorter, select the slides whose titles you want to use.

Click the Summary Slide button. PowerPoint creates the agenda slide, with titles from the selected slides.

To create an interactive agenda slide

Create a PowerPoint presentation as you like. Do not create the agenda or overview slide. Next you will create a custom show for each topic that you want to include on the agenda slide. A custom show is a sub-group of slides within a presentation. Custom shows can be quite useful when you want to create one presentation for multiple audiences. Consider the following example.

Presentation Topics	*Custom Shows*
Dogs	Custom Show 1 (Dogs)
Labrador Retrievers	Labrador Retrievers
Italian Greyhounds	Italian Greyhounds
Welsh Terriers	Welsh Terriers
Cats Custom Show 2 (Cats)	
Siamese	Siamese
Maltese	Maltese
Manx	Manx
Fish Custom Show 3 (Fish)	
Guppy	Guppy
Grouper	Grouper
Garibaldi	Garibaldi

Create a custom show for each topic you want on the agenda slide. Include all topics within the custom show.

— On the Slide Show menu, select Custom Shows. The Custom Shows dialog appears.

— Click New. The Define Custom Show dialog appears. All of the slides contained in the presentation are listed on the left: the slides in the custom show are listed on the right.

— Select the slides to include in the first custom show. Use the Add button to add the slides.

— When you are finished, click OK. The Custom Show dialog reappears.

— Continue creating custom shows for each sub-group of slides that you want to create. When you are finished, click Close.

Now that the presentation contains custom shows, you are ready to create the agenda slide.

— Go to the PowerPoint Slide Sorter (so that you can view all of the slides in the presentation).

— Select the first slide in each custom show (Shift + select slides).

— Click the Summary Slide button. PowerPoint creates the agenda slide, with titles from the selected slides.

— Select the agenda slide, and then switch to Slide view (so that you view only this slide).

Now you can create the hyperlinks from the items on the agenda slide to their respective slides.

— Select (highlight) the agenda item.

— From the Slide Show menu, select Action Settings.

— Select Hyperlink to. Then, select Custom Shows from the drop-down listbox.

— Choose the desired Custom Show.

— Select Show and Return, and then click OK.

— Complete all necessary steps for each item on the agenda slide.

RUNNING POWERPOINT PRESENTATIONS ON 2 MONITORS (OR USING A PROJECTOR AND A MONITOR)

If you have ever wanted to run a PowerPoint slide show

and edit it at the same time, you will be pleased with PowerPoint! PowerPoint has a new feature that supports the dual-monitor capabilities built into Windows® 98 and Windows 2000. If you have a computer with two monitors (or a monitor and a projector), you can run a slide show and edit a presentation at the same time. Best of all, you view the whole presentation, (including speaker notes), while the audience sees only the slides. You can even make changes to the presentation on the fly — without ever exiting the slide show. This is a wonderful feature for anyone in a truly interactive environment.

The dual-monitor feature lets you set up one monitor to display the main PowerPoint window and the second monitor (or projector) to display a full-screen slide show. Once you've configured this setup, you can run the slide show on one monitor, and view or edit the presentation on the other. Each screen behaves as it normally would. You move from one monitor to the other by moving the mouse.

The dual-monitor feature lets you do the following:

— *View your outline, slides, and speaker notes in:* Normal view while the audience sees only slides Normal view is the new default view for editing presentations in PowerPoint 2000. The three panes in this view let you see your slides, outline, and notes at the same time. When you display your presentation in Normal view on one monitor, you can see the slide that your audience sees, as well as your notes and outline.

— *View upcoming slides and speaker notes without advancing the slide show:* In Normal view, you can move around in the presentation to see upcoming slides and speaker notes without advancing the slide show on the second monitor. When you do advance the slide show by moving the mouse to the second monitor and clicking, the presentation in Normal view on the first monitor is automatically re-synchronised to match.

— *Modify your presentation on the fly:* You can edit your presentation on one monitor while the slide show is displayed on the other.

— *Keep the Meeting Minder window available without distracting your audience:* The Meeting Minder window lets you record action items and meeting minutes during a slide show.

To run a Slide Show and edit a presentation at the same time in PowerPoint

Your system must be configured for two monitors. If your system is already configured for two monitors, PowerPoint automatically displays the slide show on the second monitor when you start a slide show. (You can use the procedure "Set up PowerPoint to run on two monitors" to change the monitor that displays the slide show.) If your system is not yet configured for two monitors, complete the following steps. First, configure the system to recognise more than one monitor. Then, set up PowerPoint to run on two monitors.

Skipping Slides Using the Slide Navigator in PowerPoint

We all start out our presentations with good intentions. In ideal situations we write, design, and test our presentations. We make sure they are geared for the proper audience and timed well. However, the real world often throws us curves . . .

The audience is restless, and they don't seem to want to sit still for the entire presentation — you need to skip some of the slides, but you don't want the audience to know you are doing so . . .

Someone in the audience raises a question, and you have the perfect slide for explanation — but that is Slide #12, and you are on Slide #4 . . .

Even better, you expect to deliver a presentation that raises some questions about the value of the Sales Group, and you don't expect the Director of Sales Marketing to attend in the presentation — yet halfway through the presentation, in she walks, right before you are to reveal the "less-than-respectful" slide . . .

UGH! What do you do?

In any of these situations, you can find creative ways to skip slides. You can simply turn off your electronic presentation and cover the rest of the material without visual aids. You can even attempt to skip around the presentation, darting to the slide you want to view or sliding past the one you want to omit. But isn't there a better solution to this slightly ad hoc manner of navigating through a presentation?

Fortunately, yes there is: you can use the Slide Navigator tool in PowerPoint.

To skip to a slide out of sequence using the Slide Navigator in PowerPoint

Open a PowerPoint presentation in Slide Show mode. (Select View > Slide Show or click the Slide Show button in the lower left corner.)

Navigate through the presentation as desired.

When you are ready to jump to a slide other than the next one in the presentation, right-click anywhere on the screen. (Or, left-click in the box in the bottom left corner.) The Slide Show popup menu appears.

Select Go > Slide Navigator. The Slide Navigator dialog appears.

In the Slide titles list box, double-click the slide title you want to show. (Or, select the slide title and click Go To.) The Slide Show continues — jumping directly to the slide you selected. It advances from this slide forward. If you skipped slides, they are not shown at all — unless you return to the Slide Navigator and select the slides.

Recording Action Items While Delivering PowerPoint Presentations

Have you ever been in the middle of delivering a presentation . . . everything is going well, people are really contributing to the discussion, ideas are flying, and the group comes up with a list of items that need to be investigated further? Maybe it's a list of things that need to be accomplished; maybe it's a few related items that need to be discussed at a later date. In any case, if you are delivering the presentation, what can you do?

You can grab a pen and start trying to write down things while you are still delivering the presentation; you can ask someone else to do the same. Either way — the flow of the presentation is lost . . . So why not use the technology you are using for the presentation to help you? You can use PowerPoint to take down action items and assign responsible parties. It's really quite simple to do.

Open a PowerPoint presentation in Slide Show mode. Select View > Slide Show or click the Slide Show button in the lower left corner.

Navigate through the presentation as desired.

When you are ready to take notes or assign an action item to someone, right-click anywhere on the screen. (Or, left-click in the box in the bottom left corner.)

Select Meeting Minder . . . from the list of options. The Meeting Minder dialog appears. In this case, let's assume in the course of delivering the presentation, you have come up with several action items that need to be resolved. You want to make a list of these items (and assign owners) during the presentation so you don't forget about them.

Select the Action Items tab.

Enter a Description for the task.

In the Assigned To field, enter an individual or department's name. Enter a Due Date.

Click Add.

There are two additional options on this dialog: Schedule and Export. You don't need to select either of these options, but they can be useful.

- *Schedule:* Clicking this option launches MS Outlook (if it is installed) and allows you to schedule an appointment or meeting about this action item on the fly.
- *Export*: Clicking this option allows you to Post action items to MS Outlook or Send meeting minutes and action items to MS Word. Click Cancel to return to the previous dialog.

Click OK to return to the presentation in progress.

Best of all, when you get to the last slide in the presentation, a new slide will appear. This slide lists the action items captured during the presentation.

You can use this slide as a way to wrap up the presentation or simply leave it projected after the presentation ends. If you don't want to show the slide at all — just remember to end your presentation with the original "final" slide.

Using Keyboard Shortcuts in PowerPoint

Keyboard shortcuts are a great way to save time and effort. Shortcut keys can help you bypass menus and carry out commands directly. In fact, when creating text-heavy presentations, it is often quite easy to do almost everything with the keyboard — instead of using the mouse. (You can save the mouse for drawing items.)

The only trick to keyboard shortcuts is memorising them. Fortunately, you can access the complete list of keyboard shortcuts by using the Microsoft Office Assistant. In PowerPoint (or any of the other Office 2000 applications), just press F1 to display the Assistant. Type "shortcut keys" in the text box.

Here are some of the most useful PowerPoint shortcut keys:

Action	*Shortcut Keys*
Open a PowerPoint presentation	Ctrl + O
Insert a new slide	Ctrl + M
Copy	Ctrl + C
Paste	Ctrl + V
Save	Ctrl + S
Print	Ctrl + P
Bold	Ctrl + B
Italicize	Ctrl + I
Capitalise	Shift + F3
Apply subscript	Ctrl + = (Equal Sign)
Apply superscript	Ctrl + + (Plus Sign)
Find	Ctrl + F
Select all	Ctrl + A

Delete word	Ctrl + Backspace
Repeat last action	F4 or Ctrl + Y
Insert hyperlink	Ctrl + K
Promote paragraph	Alt + Shift + Left Arrow
Demote paragraph	Alt + Shift + Right Arrow
View guides	Ctrl + G
Make duplicate slide	Ctrl + D
Start slide show	F5

Creating Handouts in PowerPoint

Many presenters use PowerPoint's "Notes" feature to create speaker notes. Did you know that you can also use these notes to create detailed handouts for an audience? You can create custom handouts from speaker notes. These notes can contain slides and notes, slides only, or notes only. It's all up to you!

To create handouts

Open the PowerPoint presentation.

From the View menu, select Master > Handout Master.

Select the desired layout on the Handout Master toolbar.

From the File menu, select Print.

In the Print dialog, select the number of slides you want to appear on the handout. Then, click OK.

Creating Speaker Notes in PowerPoint

Many presenters like to use notes that go along with their PowerPoint slides. These notes can be printed and used for reference or combined with their related slides to create handouts for an audience.

To create a Master Notes page

If you have text to appear on all notes pages, simply create a master page and enter the appropriate text.

Open the PowerPoint presentation.

From the View menu, select Master > Notes Master.

Optional: You can change the location of the slide image or notes box if desired. Simply click on the slide or text box and drag to the desired location.

Optional: Add text, header, footer, date, etc. as desired.

From the View menu, select the desired viewing option.

To add Speaker Notes

Open the PowerPoint presentation.

From the View menu, select Notes Page.

Select the notes box at the bottom of the page. Enter notes for the current slide.

Use the scroll bar to navigate through slides.

Adding Comments (Redlines) to PowerPoint Presentations

Often, when you review a presentation (whether created by you or by someone else), you need to make edits. If you are like many people, you play the presentation (using Slide Show) and scribble down notes on a piece of paper.

There is an easier way of communicating.

PowerPoint allows you to insert comments directly on the slides. The comments appear in yellow comment boxes, and you can move, resize, and reformat the text and comment boxes just as you can any other object.

To add comments to a presentation

Open a PowerPoint presentation.

Left-click the presentation Slide Show button.

While viewing the presentation, right-click and then select Pointer Options > Pen.

Hold down the mouse button as you write or draw on a slide.

Printing Colour Slides in Black and White in PowerPoint

Most presentations are designed to be shown in colour, but the presentation handouts or other supporting materials that are created from the presentation are usually printed in black and white. As a result of this difference, things that look fabulous on the projected screen may not appear so fabulous when printed. For example, filled objects or dithered backgrounds that look good on the screen can make printed handouts unreadable.

To print a presentation in black and white

Open the presentation in PowerPoint.

From the View menu, select Black and White.

PowerPoint changes the slide display so that you can see a grayscale preview of how the slides will look when printed in black and white.

To customise this display, right-click in Slide view. Select Black and White and the desired option. For example, Automatic only shows text and graphics: it hides a textured or shaded background.

To print a presentation in pure black and white

You can also print a presentation in pure black and white. This hides all shades of gray, including object fills.

Open the presentation in PowerPoint.

From the File menu, select Print.

Select Black and White and click OK.

Spell Checking PowerPoint Presentations Not in English

Follow these easy steps to make sure your presentation is perfect — regardless of its language.

To select the language in which to spellcheck

Open the PowerPoint presentation.

Select the text to spellcheck.

From the Tools menu, select Language.

Select the desired language and click OK.

From the Tools menu, select Spelling. PowerPoint locates any misspelled words.

To change the default language dictionary

Open the PowerPoint presentation.

From the Tools menu, select Language.

Select the desired language and click Default.

Creating Custom Dictionaries in Microsoft Word

Most presentation applications have extensive text

creation and editing abilities. Microsoft PowerPoint, for example, allows you to work in an Outline view that looks just like the Microsoft Word interface. You can add and edit text as easily as you can in Word. You can even access many advanced word processing features like — drag and drop editing, spelling, and cut and paste. (In PowerPoint, just use the Tools menu item and click Options. The Edit and Spelling tabs contain several good word processing features.)

Nevertheless, the best editing options in presentation applications are not as extensive as they are in Word. Additionally, many people simply feel more comfortable "writing" in Word. Consequently, it is not at all unusual to write an initial draft of presentation content in Word and then copy the content into a presentation application like PowerPoint.

While this is an unnecessary step in many cases, it does allow you to access certain Word features that are really wonderful tools . . . one of these is the Custom Dictionary option in Word.

The Custom Dictionary allows you to store your own dictionary in Word — one with words YOU use again and again. This is a wonderful tool if you frequently write about an industry or product with unique terms or individual names — items that would not likely be contained in a traditional dictionary. Best of all, it is easy to create a custom dictionary. In fact, if you are using Word now, you probably have the beginning of a custom dictionary already started.

The PowerPoint Viewer

The PowerPoint Viewer is a program used to run slide shows on computers that don't PowerPoint installed. You can add the Viewer to the disk that contains the presentation using Pack and Go Wizard. Then, you can unpack the Viewer and presentation together and run the slide show on another computer. You can even create a play list to use with the Viewer so you can run multiple presentations, one after another.

To pack up a presentation for use on a computer that does not contain PowerPoint

Open the presentation you want to save to a disk.

Select File > Pack and Go.

Follow the instructions in the Pack and Go Wizard. If the presentation contains linked files or TrueType fonts, you can choose your presentation.

When you are prompted, select to include the PowerPoint Viewer.

Finish running the Wizard.

To unpack the presentation to run on another computer

Insert the disk on which you copied the presentation and Viewer.

In Windows Explorer, go to the drive where the disk is located: double click Pngsetup.

Enter the destination to which you want to copy the presentation.

To run the slide show, double-click the PowerPoint Viewer — Ppview.

Select the presentation you want to run. Then, select any desired options.

Click Show.

Jumping to the Internet from PowerPoint Presentations

PowerPoint makes it easy to do all sorts of things through the use of actions buttons. You simply add an action button to a presentation. Then, you define how to use this button during the slide show. Consider the following options:

— Jump from one presentation to another without closing the first one

— Jump to a slide not contained in order

— Start a movie

— Go to an Internet address

To jump to an Internet address from a PowerPoint presentation

This example reveals how easy it is to add a jump to an Internet site to a PowerPoint presentation.

Open the PowerPoint presentation.

Navigate to the slide to which you want to add the action button.

On the Drawing toolbar, select Auto Shapes.

Select Action Buttons and select the desired button. You can choose any button.

Click to place the button on the slide. The Action Settings dialog appears. This is the dialog in which you determine the button action.

Select the Mouse Click tab.

Under Action on click, select Hyperlink to and then choose URL from the drop-down listbox.

In the Hyperlink to URL dialog, enter the site address and click OK.

Click OK again to insert the button.

8

DO'S AND DON'TS OF POSTER PRESENTATION

Good science, uncluttered and colourful design, legibility, brevity of text, and straightforward organisation equal a good poster. New and exciting ideas based on sound research can draw deserved recognition through a well-written abstract and an eye-catching poster design. Scientists must recognise that participants at a scientific meeting may not have had the opportunity to read the abstract of a poster presentation before they walk into the display area. Attention will invariably be drawn to posters with a crisp, clean design and a snappy title. The title must have the audience in mind. It helps to think of a title as a newspaper headline vying for attention. Once the viewer has come to take a closer look at an interesting-looking display, all aspects of the design and the science work together to keep, or lose, the viewer's attention.

Does your business suddenly encounter the need for printing posters? Before running to the nearest poster printing company you can find, it is suggested that you do the stop and think routine first.

Your budget could be saved a lot more if you come to the poster printing suppliers fully knowledgeable of the features, benefits and designs of an effective poster. You must be definite on the custom printed poster you will need depending on your objectives for it.

PRINCIPLES OF POSTER DESIGN

Posters are replacing short, submitted, oral "papers" at large meetings of scientific societies. Gluts of submitted papers have caused meetings to have so many concurrent paper-reading sessions that the supply of meeting rooms is strained and attendees find it impossible to be in the correct room at the correct time for each of numerous papers they may wish to hear. Under these circumstances, many attendees decide their time is best spent in symposia, where invited experts give longer papers relevant to subjects selected because of their importance to members. These factors cause poor attendance at submitted-paper sessions and an increasing emphasis on poster sessions-in which the audience wanders among the displays, finding posters of interest and holding one-on-one discussions with the presenters. Most presenters find this more satisfying than talking to a nearly empty room.

— *Posters are not oral presentations.* Your poster should be self-explanatory. You will probably be present during only part of the time your poster is available for viewing. Furthermore, while you are on station and discussing your poster with one viewer, other viewers may wish to ascertain your poster's message and move on. Therefore, posters are NOT the assembled, printed-out images (slides or "screens") that were prepared for an oral presentation.

— *Posters are not manuscripts.* Posters need supporting text, but the text should be restricted to making the most important points. Viewers will not wish to stand at your poster and spend many minutes reading. If you have extensive text that you wish viewers to access, make a handout that the viewer can take from a pouch attached at the bottom right of the display board.

— *Posters are visual displays.* Effective posters have a series of brief statements and supporting illustrations that tell a story. If your display is drab, overly complex, or not easy to follow, viewers will likely move on rather than sampling or learning your poster's message.

Poster Contexts

Poster sessions. When a poster session is part of a scientific meeting, those organising the session generally provide boards of a stated size (a common size used to be 4 × 8 ft. or 3 × 6 ft. in landscape orientation, but to more effectively use display space, 3 × 4 ft. portrait orientation is now the norm) onto which participants mount the items that make up their display. Other features of the boards, such as colour, hardness, and texture, may not be known until the presenter enters the exhibit hall to arrange his/her display. Even when the presenter has been told what to expect, last-minute changes sometimes occur for reasons beyond the control of the organiser of the poster session. For example, the surface colour and hardness of the boards may be different than advertised or the 3 × 6 ft. display boards may be oriented vertically rather than horizontally.

Other contexts. When a poster is not for an announced poster session, you will likely be required to provide some means of support as it stands on the floor or on a table, in a lobby or the periphery of a meeting room. Self-supporting poster displays are more difficult to prepare and to transport than are displays attached to boards provided by those organising a poster session. However, you have control of all features of the poster-not just the items that will be displayed.

STEPS TO DESIGN A POSTER

Have a Plan

Decide upon the message of your poster and plan the items that will develop and deliver this message in a logical and visually appealing manner. Get ideas for design, colour, and visual effects from other posters and from the display ads on billboards and in magazines.

Keep the design simple and as uncluttered as possible.

Sketch out your ideas on paper or use a scaled planning sheet as a guide.

Show the flow!

It is important that the viewer know in what order you wish the parts of your poster to be viewed. Without guidance from you, the viewer will start at upper left and work either down or to the right. Use arrows, numbers, or letters to help the onlooker follow the viewing sequence you planned.

Third Dimension

Any item that projects from the generally flat surface of a poster will attract attention. Examples include pictures or maps mounted on foam board, a piece of research equipment, shallow plexiglas cages with live insects, a stack of 3.5" diskettes, a book, and half of a longitudinally cut cup, vial, or small log.

Tips on Poster Parts

Colour coordination

If you don't have good colour sense, get help from

someone who does. Choosing colours that go together is an important part of preparing a pleasing poster.

Poster title

The title of the display and the name(s) of the author(s) should be given at the top of your display. To command the attention that it deserves, it should be in larger Because the heading will likely be longer than landscape-oriented legal paper (14"), it must be pieced together from 11 or 14" segments or specially printed. OIR Photography and Graphics will print one to your specifications.

Text

All text should be 18 point or larger, so that it can be read 1 to 2 metres away, where viewers are likely to stand. Headings should be larger yet. Use colour and/or bold fonts sparingly to emphasise your major points or to call attention to captions.

Typographic tips for blocks of text

Serif fonts are more readable than are sans serif fonts but not as legible. Either may be used for blocks of text.

Avoid using all capital letterss. Other methods, including colour, are more effective for emphasis.

Don't crowd text. Don't be afraid of "white space"; it can make your poster more attractive.

Use hyphens sparingly or not at all

Justify text only if the lines are long enough to avoid unseemly gaps between words.

Typographic tips for headings

Headings should catch the reader's eye and arouse

interest in your message. They should therefore be concise, arresting, and informative. Sans serif fonts are more legible than serif fonts and are appropriate to headings.

Don't hyphenate headings.

Break lines intelligently.

Tables

Tables should be kept simple and used sparingly. Graphs are generally a more effective means of displaying data. Use 24-point lettering or larger for tabular data. Use colour and/or bold fonts for data you wish to emphasise.

Graphs, photographs, maps, drawings, etc.

These should be made large enough to view at 1 to 2 metres. Their relevance should be evident without the viewer having to read paragraphs of text. Photographs should be in colour and can be photographic enlargements, xerographic enlargements of slides, or ink-jet prints of scanned originals.

Background

The items you prepare for your poster will look best if displayed against a background that contrasts pleasingly with their colours. If you are to attach them to a board provided by others, you may not know what colour or texture that background will be. You may overcome this limitation to colour coordinating your poster by bringing your own background material, either cloth or paper of the colour(s) you select. If you bring your own background, make sure you can install it without it showing unsightly creases, wrinkles, or folds.

Here are some suggestions that will make a poster more accessible, attractive, and interesting.

1. At first glance from 3-4 m away the viewer should see an easy-to-read title and an uncluttered, neat arrangement of photos and/or illustrations and text. It should be obvious where to start inspecting the poster and where to go from there (generally left to right, top to bottom). As this progression is vital, the component parts should either be numbered to facilitate this or have arrows that graphically lead the viewer through the display.
2. Use elements of different sizes and proportions. Same-size and same-proportioned components result in a boring design. For particular emphasis, try using different shapes.
3. A large and/or bright center of interest can draw the eye to the most important aspect of the poster-a simplified, bold cross section illustrating a structural feature, a colourful paleogeographic map, a blowup of a photo of a new species, or a large outcrop photo illustrating depositional environments. Colour poster prints, 30 x 46 cm or 50 x 76 cm, from photographic slides or negatives can be ordered for a modest price at most photo shops. Smaller images (e.g., 20 x 30 cm) can be printed on a colour inkjet or laser printer.
4. Enlarge all photos enough for pertinent details to be clearly evident.
5. Make all illustrations simple and bold. Leave out any unnecessary detail in the story being presented.
6. Convert tabular data to a graphic display, if possible. Try scatter plots, polar plots, bar graphs, or triangular diagrams.
7. Consider the inclusion of (small) rock or fossil specimens on the poster. They can be fastened to poster board with silicone glue.

8. Make a scale drawing of your layout. Have a few colleagues comment on the overall design before final drafting. If you have access to professional drafting personnel, ask for their suggestions.
9. The main tenet of good poster design is simplicity.

Lettering, line weights, and colour; computer printouts

All lettering should be legible from 2 m away; older viewers should not have to put on reading glasses. The minimum type size should be no less than 18 points, and the style should be bold or semi-bold in simple, clean-looking type:

— This is 18 point type, the smallest size you should use.You should be able to read it from 2 metres away.

— This is 24 point type. Better?

The title lettering should be the largest, about 5-8 cm (144-288 points), with subheadings 1-3 cm (36-72 points) high. If you don't use a computer, office and art supply stores have a wide variety of stick-on and rub-on individual letters in various colours and sizes which are ideal for titles and subheadings. For material other than titles and subheadings, capitals and lower-case letters in combination are much easier to read than all capitals:

Most print in newspapers, magazines, and books is in lower-case letters (except for the capitalisation of proper names and the initial word in a sentence). Lower-case letters generally are regarded as much easier to recognise than words printed only in capitalised letters.

Most print in newspapers, magazines, and books is in lower-case letters (except for the capitalisation of proper names and the initial word in a sentence). Lower-case letters generally are regarded as much easier to recognise than words printed only in capitalised letters.

Again, if you do not use a computer, text material can be typed at about 12 points, then enlarged on a copying machine to as large as 24 points without significant loss of clarity:

— of the Quaternary (12 points)

— of the Quaternary (24 points)

The typed material may also be enlarged photographically. A professional appearance can be obtained by use of a lettering machine that produces strips of stick-on text. These lines of text, in the final size, are applied to plain white paper and then photographed so that the tape does not show.

Both typed lettering and stick-on lettering can be combined with black and white line drawings before the final copy (copy machine enlargement or photographic enlargement) is made. Line drawings (e.g., maps, diagrams, fossils, cross-sections) should use a line weight that will be no thinner than 0.7 mm in the final product. Bolder lines are preferable. Keep the drawing simple and leave out all extraneous details.

When applying colour, some authors prefer soft, muted tones; others like deep or very bright ones. The temptation is to use colour everywhere, but don't. The viewer's eye will jump erratically around the poster instead of tracking through it to the crucial points. The less important parts of the poster-the necessary background information, the supporting data-will seem to recede into the background if done in cool or cool-neutral colours. The featured parts can be highlighted by using warm colours, or black if the background colours are soft, or white if the background colours are bright or deep. In choosing colours be aware that lighting in the display area may not be optimal.

Colour is easy to apply to illustrations that are drafted on a computer using a standard drawin programme (e.g.,

Illustrator, Freehand, Canvas, Corel Draw). Such programmes provide the opportunity of selecting from millions of colours, and adjusting hue, chroma, and value so they are most effective. When drafting illustrations without a computer, colour can be applied to black and white drawings after they are photocopied, unless the cost of colour printing is no object. Transparent or opaque sheets of stick-on colour (use non-glare, matte-finish type) provide the most even shading. Coloured stick-on tape comes in widths up to 5 cm. The flexible kind can be used for line work. The standard kind is perfect for bar graphs and histograms, for borders, and as leaders from one element of the poster to another. Coloured stick-on dots, squares, and triangles are available in various sizes. Large arrows can be cut from stick-on tape or from stick-on colour sheets.

Text

The text material included on a poster should be extremely brief, or most of the audience will walk away. Some authors like to include the full abstract as part of the poster, but they should not rely on its being read. More successful is placement of a succinct statement of major conclusions at the beginning of the poster- perhaps as an expanded subtitle. The supporting text is then presented in brief segments along with appropriate illustrations, and the significance of the findings is made forcefully and concisely at the end. Aim for "Wow!" from the viewer. Handouts of the abstract may be made available for interested viewers.

MOUNTING, PACKAGING, DISPLAYING

Those preparing a poster with a computer program should be able to design the entire poster in a single file and print it on a large-output printer that will handle documents with dimensions of a meter or more. In this case, you can simply role up the printed posted and carry it to the meeting in a packing tube.

For those preparing individual poster elements for later assembly, each element should be mounted with an adhesive on poster board or on 1/8" foam-core board so that they will lie flat. A clean look is achieved if the caption is mounted on the same board as the accompanying illustration. A half inch or so of the coloured poster board extending beyond the edge of an illustration effectively frames it. Select the mounting colour carefully so that it does not overpower the picture. Illustrations mounted on the white foam-core board can be edged with coloured stick-on tape.

If you know you will be flying to the meeting, carry the poster with you. Make poster elements small enough that they can be included with your carry-on-baggage (dimensions generally 44 x 56 cm; call the airline to be sure) to avoid the problem of lost checked luggage. You may have only a short time to set up your display, so prepare for this in advance. Have these items in a poster emergency kit: tape measure, 3 m length of string, box of clear push-pins (get longer than standard ones if mounted illustrations are thicker than 3 mm or a box of dressmakers' round-headed pins, ordinary thumb tacks, roll of double-stick tape, scissors, glue, package of tissue paper. Have a sketch of the poster layout, with positions of a few key components measured off so you know where to place them. Set up a level line, if needed, by tying the string between two push-pins set a measured distance above the bottom of the display board. The poster elements can be fastened to the board without visible attachments, as shown below, or can be attached with the push-pins (or dressmakers' pins), or with lots of double-stick tape.

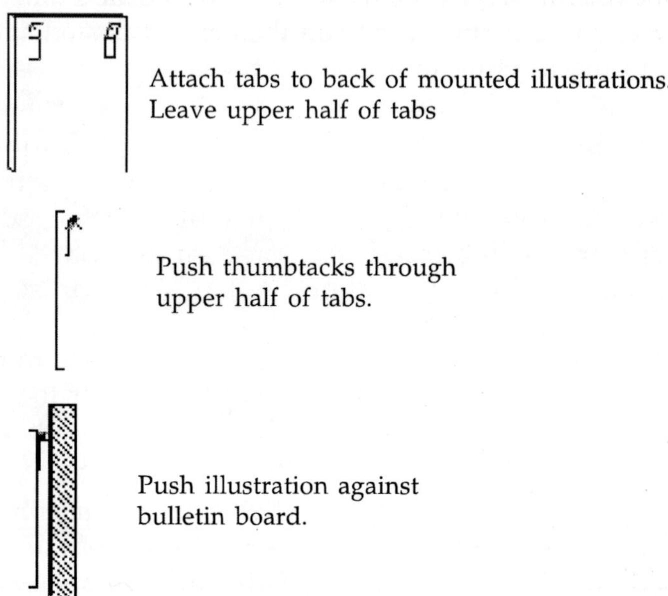

When you remove the display, if you've used double-stick tape, put a sheet of tissue paper between the components when stacking them to keep them from sticking together.

CUSTOM PRINTED POSTERS

Posters are flexible advertising tools they are intended to catch more mobile viewers. Poster sizes range from 81/2 x 11 to 19 x 27 depending on the amount of contents and graphics. Poster printing companies vary on the paper stock used to print posters. They usually range from 80# or 100#.

Benefits of Custom Printed Posters

There are numerous uses for posters and as such, there are also numerous benefits in using them. It can publicise events to take place. Posters can be an effective way to promote a service being offered. It can also be used in selling a product. Posters can be a trendsetter or can develop an attitude.

In order to know more about the benefits and advantages a poster can bring for your company, take note of a basic difference between posters and other advertising media. Posters, unlike other advertising and promotional materials, speak to the audience who are mobile or are "on the move". This is the main difference since newspaper ads, magazine ads and mailing pieces like brochures, flyers and pamphlets are designed for audience who has time to site and take in a lot of information. A poster can only put in a few words and graphics that should capture a viewer's attention immediately and spark them to react.

A measure of an effective poster is that audiences that are passing by would be riveted to pay attention on the message it imparts. Also, the response of the public in whatever has been advertised on a poster speaks for itself how effective it has been.

Designing Custom Printed Poster

There's a design technique called symmetry that applies well when designing your poster. Symmetry combines graphics and text to create balance in the design. The effect of the balance allows the viewer's eyes to flow from one point to another on the poster and this causes movement. Your poster achieved a good design by having both balance and movement. These poster design essentials will be the foremost factor and will give the viewer's a mental pull to pay attention, read and react to it. As much as possible make your poster eye-catching, attractive and not too crowded with information. Through this, you will have effective printed posters economically.

Once you have realised the important features and benefits of poster printing, you are equipped enough to pick out the poster printing company that will meet your demands.

ALTERNATIVE POSTER

The professional-looking poster discussed above has an attractive counterpart. The artistically inclined scientist can make a poster by sketching it entirely by hand. This approach should follow the same science and design guidelines as previously described, but the text is produced with coloured felt-tip pens on poster board of pleasing complementary or neutral colour. Text material (a minimum of 18-point type) is easy to do by hand with felt marking pens if there are lightly penciled lines to follow. This less formal type of poster is fast and inexpensive to make, and if neatly and imaginatively done can have a very special appeal.

Designing your Poster in Computer

Posters for scientific meetings are made in a number of ways, typically either from small bits and pieces that are printed separately and glued onto a backing to create panels or from larger printed sheets that include text and embedded images. While we make many 40" by 40" posters, they are printed downtown. More often we use an Epson 3000 printer to print posters that are composed of four or six panels, each of which measures 16.5" by 23.4" (42 cm by 59.4 cm).

Begin the design of your poster with a small sketch that shows the whole thing with the title block, major headings, running body text and your pictures and figures. Several iterations of thumbnail sketches will help you understand what should go where and how much space will be needed for each part.

The individual panels can be vertical but are far more often horizontal. Before you begin to assemble your poster set the page size in your software. Most computers will not list A2 as a paper size, so go to Page Setup, select custom size and specify 16" by 22.65" (40.6 cm by 57.5 cm) as the size. You should also leave margins of at least a quarter of an inch on three sides of the image area and a margin of half an inch on the bottom of your poster. Most of our posters are made in Microsoft PowerPoint, but they could also be made in Adobe Photoshop, Adobe Illustrator, Adobe InDesign or Corel Draw. PowerPoint has serious limitations for page design and does not allow precise placement of the parts of posters, but it is what most people use.

The overall design of your poster should be eye catching, easy to follow and visually appealing. People don't want to stand there reading all of Tolstoy's War and Peace so try to limit the amount of text in your poster and instead use figures where appropriate. The ratio of the golden section is used by many designers to create harmony in the relationship of the parts to each other and of the parts to the whole.

The figure to the right by the great French architect le Corbusier shows how the human body reflects the proportions of the golden section. The ratio of 1 to 1.618 repeats a number of times both in the ratio of the parts of the body to the whole and the ratios of parts of the body to each other.

These proportions can be found throughout nature and are used by many designers, painters and architects. Try to create balance and harmony in your poster by keeping this proportion in mind.

Type can be set flush left, flush right, centered and justified, but blocks of sold text are usually more readible when justified. Type can be set in a sans serif face (Arial,

Swiss or Helvetica) or a serif face and can be bolded, italicised or italicised bold. Below are examples of serif and sans serif type. The serrifs are the small cross pieces that terminate the shafts of the letters.

Well designed posters often use large bolded sans serif type (60-96 point) for the title, smaller bolded sans serif type 30-36 point) for section headings and a roman type (18 to 24 point) for the body text. Fancy faces should be avoided, since they are difficult to read and borders around blocks of text should similarly be avoided since they break up the flow of the whole. You do not have fill every bit of space. Some empty space will increase the ease of viewing.

To make you poster more readible, the colour of the type should clearly contrast with the background colour. In the following examples, notice how as contrast between text and background decreases the words become difficult and then impossible to read. Body text should never extend across the whole width of a panel of your poster. Instead, type should be broken into two or more columns to increase its readability. When possible, the panels should be designed with a grid in mind and all the elements, headings, body text and figures should be arranged on a grid. Your readers must be able to follow the flow of your text and images and the elements must line up from panel to panel. As mentioned above, make sure your text is easily readible by using light type on dark backgrounds or dark type on light backgrounds. Avoid colour schemes that require that viewers wear sunglasses.

In the poster above the white borders were cut off with a razor and when assembled into the final poster the panels were brought together giving it the appearance of one unified whole. The UVic logo should be included in your poster when possible, especially if it is to be used off campus. Below are two styles of the UVic logo. Click on either to bring up larger versions and then right click on the one you want in order to save it. Then use the Insert/ Picture/From File comand and place it in your poster

PRINTING THE POSTER

Please use your name as part of the poster file name. If you are using any unusual fonts make sure a copy accompanies your file, otherwise font substitutions may occur with strange and embarrassing consequences. If you are doing the printing yourself, feed one sheet of paper at a time, putting it glossy side down on top of a backing sheet. Go to the Print/Properties and select the Main tab. Specify the paper type as glossy photo quality paper and select quality rather than speed. On the Paper tab select the paper size as A2, select centered and set orientation to Portrait or Landscape as required. Close Print/Properties and on the Print tab select scale to fit paper. Then Print each page, one at a time.

The printer sometimes behaves badly and runs a sheet through without printing anything, in which case the paper should be carefully fed again and the printer should be unpaused or reset. Make sure that none of the ink out lights are lit. Please try to book time well in advance for when you want to print. Four panels will need as much as five hours, depending on your file size. You might want to have the finished panels laminated, otherwise they will fade and will be very susceptible to scratches and water damage.

Poster-making Tasks

Printing

Laser printers are good for black-and-white text or graphs, but a colour ink-jet printer is needed to make colourful graphs and to add colour highlights to text. Wide-format colour printing is becoming an increasingly popular way to print large portions of a poster or even the whole poster on a single sheet. However, this is presently too expensive to be an option for most posters. Colour enlargements of colour hardcopy or from colour slides can be done at most copy centres.

Lamination

Putting a film plastic film on one or both sides of poster items protects ink jet printing from the effects of wetting and makes finger prints and other marks easier to remove. Sheets of lamination plastic for 8.5 × 11" or smaller items are sold by office supply stores. Graphics shops have machines that can laminate items of all sizes.

Cutting poster board for mounting items

You can use a straight edge and a sharp knife to cut pieces of poster board on which to mount items for your poster. However, a mat cutter makes the job much easier.

Mounting items on poster board

A variety of adhesives can be used, including 3M Photo Mount™, glue sticks, and rubber cement. Whatever adhesive you use, you can improve the permanence of the bond by rolling the surface with a rubber roller.

Transporting your poster or poster parts

If you can, make all items to be displayed small enough or foldable enough to fit in your luggage. If you must transport pieces too large for that, you may need to buy or borrow an artist's portfolio. Recent changes in airline security may mean that you cannot travel with your poster if it is a heavy protective tube. Check with the airline before you fly.

Attaching items to the surface provided

If you have your own background material for a poster, your first job is to attach it to the display board. This may not be easy. The surface will be immovably vertical, and you may have to attach and stretch single-handedly a very large piece of material. Some display boards are so hard that inserting a push pin or thumbtack is difficult.

Others are so soft, that a short thumbtack may be insufficient to hold up a heavy item. Hard surfaces require short, firm fasteners that can be hammered in. Soft surfaces require longer fasteners that can be pushed in deeply. Velcro fasteners are quick and convenient, but may not attach to some surfaces.Come prepared with fasteners for all contingencies, and remember you will need to remove them as well as insert them. Meetings usually do NOT provide fasteners nor the tools to deal with them. Poster tool kit. You should take with you the items you may need to assemble and take down your poster at a scientific meeting-such as, fasteners (velcro strips, map pins, small nails, etc.), small hammer, pliers, scissors, 2-sided tape, and transparent mending tape.

PREPARING DIGITAL POSTERS

The proliferation of poster presentation sessions at scientific meetings and conferences has grown in response to exponential advances in contemporary research in science, technology and medicine. During the past thirty years, the need to communicate, disseminate, document and preserve new research has outstripped the capacity of scientific sessions at scholarly meetings and conferences. As a result, posters have evolved into the third leg of a scholarly publication tripod, joining abstracts and published papers in journals as an essential component of scientific communications.

For example, one of the largest organisers of scientific information, the American Heart Association, first began considering poster sessions as an effective and inexpensive technique for presenting research only in 1974 when requests for simultaneous traditional sessions exceeded conference space and time constraints. In 1976, the AHA approved poster sessions on a one-year trial basis and 180 abstracts were accepted, on the basis of scientific merit, as posters. In 2000, nearly 50 percent of abstracts, or about 3,000 posters were approved and presented at AHA's annual scientific conference.

The majority of scientific posters today are still assembled and displayed using the same cut and paste techniques used for the past three decades, but digital design, production and printing services for posters will no doubt grow in popularity in years to come. Digital alternatives have become surprisingly affordable and offer many advantages over do-it-yourself techniques. Digital production processes circumvent the complex spatial and proportional design issues inherent in hand assembly, producing posters that are more professional looking, more convenient to transport, and easier to reproduce in small sizes for handouts than traditional cut and paste methods. Presentations produced in this manner are ready to archive and disseminate electronically as well.

The guidelines presented here are meant to offer hints and tips for the preparation of posters using the digital production and printing process. Although digital poster preparation eliminates the need to be one's own designer or art director, there are some basic principles to consider in order to create an effective presentation of information about important research on serious topics. Many of the principles presented here address special considerations specific to the utilisation of digital graphic arts technology, but these guidelines also contain aesthetic and practical suggestions that can be applied to all preparation and production techniques.

Poster Design Objectives

As visual explanations, scientific posters need to be judged by their presentation as well as their content. As concise communication tools used in presentations given to small groups of people in short informal and interactive sessions, posters also need to attract viewers and provoke curiosity. Effective poster design addresses these purposes through the proper arrangement of information, graphical elegance and clear representations of complex data.

In poster construction, this involves the elements of text, graphics and tables. Although different mechanisms, they have a single purpose - the presentation of information about useful and important research on serious topics.

Making efficient and convincing summaries of data are difficult tasks, but the process can be managed by recognising that the clarity of the presentation stems from the proper arrangement of information and that graphical elegance is often found in simplicity of design and complexity of data.

Poster Design

Conventional wisdom might conclude that because scientific posters offer concise visual explanations of complex research that it is best to reduce the quantity of detail and simplify data. But the fact is that the quantity of detail and texture of the data is an issue completely separate from difficulty in reading. Clutter and confusion are failures of design and not attributes of information. Poster displays portray complexity and intricacy because the content is complex and intricate.

Effective posters are both accessible (viewer friendly) and rich in detail. They are simple in design, avoiding excessive content-free decoration, but complex in data. They may be simple but they never patronise their audience.

Here is a set of tips to make posters accessible

— The poster size should meet conference guidelines for size and content

— The title of a poster should state the conclusion of the investigation rather than the process of what was done

— The heading should include the authors' names and affiliations

— Lettering for titles should be readable from at least 6 feet away - use no less than 1-inch high type

— Words should be spelled out, avoiding mysterious abbreviations to decode

— Words should run from left to right

— The text, tables and graphics should look integrated. The same typeface should be used for all and ruled lines separating different types of information should be avoided

— Type should be in upper and lower case in a sans serif face (e.g., Arial) that is clear, precise and modes

— Lines of text should contain about 10 to 12 words

— Lettering for text in the body of the poster should be readable from at least 4 feet away - use no less than ½ inch high type

— Colour should be used sparingly and not with great contrast

— Tables are preferable to graphics for small data sets

— Tables also work well when data presentation requires many localised comparisons

— Explanations should be used to enhance access to the richness of data and make graphics more attractive to the viewer

— Words and illustrations should go together - tables and graphics should be integrated within the text whenever possible, avoiding clumsy diverting segregation

— Lines in data graphics should be thin

— Graphics should tend toward the horizontal, greater in length than height, ideally 50 percent wider than tall

— Elaborately coded shadings, cross-hatching and colours should be avoided

— Little messages help explain data. Labels should be placed on the graphics itself, no legend is required.

Digital Preparation and Printing Service

Although there are many digital printing options available, it is always best to use a service specialising in the communication of scientific information. These specialists usually offer templates that mirror the scientific process, understand poster session presentation protocol, and are able to recognise glitches that occur when sending and translating software programs, especially confusion over scientific notation.

Additional suggestions using digital processes

— Make sure the graphic arts service has upload/file transfer capabilities. Attaching graphic elements to e-mail often outstrips the capacity of many servers

— Make sure you inform your graphics arts service the platform you produced your files in. (i.e. PC or MAC). This will decrease chances of translation problems

— When using fonts other than System fonts be sure to include the original font files otherwise you may end up with a default System font

— Make sure that your images and logos are not taken from the Internet. The reproductive resolution of Web images is generally too poor for high-quality, large-format printing.

— Supply original images whenever possible. Images embedded in presentation or word processor programs may limit the ability to enlarge your figures

— Make sure the service offers electronic approvals via electronic files that can easily be sent to you via e-mail

— When checking for approval, make certain to read your text thoroughly. It is not uncommon for design software to mistranslate symbols when importing from other file formats

— Make sure that the service offers to explain screen colour versus printing colour differences to avoid surprises in the finished poster

Make sure to handle your images with care. When scanning images, coffee stains, tears and rips will reproduce. An effective poster is a marvelous communication vehicle, essentially transforming rich, dynamic and multidimensional work onto a flat 4-foot by 8-foot surface. Telling a logical narrative with a simple design and complex data can transport, inform and delight viewers in ways that can't be conveyed even with a published paper or abstract. Properly executed, the scientific poster becomes a visual experience that repays over and over again.

9

HOW TO DELIVER A GOOD PRESENTATION

ANALYSING AN AUDIENCE

One of the keys to developing effective presentations is learning how to analyse an audience—before you ever begin speaking. For example, assume you are speaking to a sales team who has just gone through a rough quarter. If you are aware of this fact before you write your presentation, you can include the type of information that would be most helpful, and avoid the kind of information that would be most harmful.

Presenters learn about their audiences from a variety of sources. Consider doing the following before a presentation:

— Interview the organisation/company executives in charge of the meeting/event

— Interview a sampling of the audience members

— Review company/organisation literature

— Research company/industry news via the Internet, magazines, newspapers, etc.

— Research associates within the industry

More importantly, try to answer the following questions in an effort to learn as much as possible about your audience.

1. Who is in Your Audience?

In order to give an effective presentation, you need to know as much as possible about your audience. Find out key demographics of the audience and determine how familiar they are with the subject of your presentation.

2. What does Your Audience Want?

One goal of your presentation is to meet the expectations of your audience. So, focus on the audience's wants and needs. The success of your presentation depends on your ability to address those wants and needs.

3. Why are you Presenting?

As you learn more about your audience and their expectations, it is important to do a self-evaluation as well. Are you comfortable speaking to this audience about this subject? Are you the right person for the presentation? How can you prepare to "be" the right person?

4. When/Where is Your Presentation?

Many presenters forget this step. Time and place are important considerations to consider when planning your presentations. Studies show that afternoon audiences respond differently than morning audiences. Typically, afternoon audiences require additional breaks because they have a reduced attention span. In addition, the venue in which you present may have a significant impact on your presentation. Presenting at a breakfast luncheon for example, requires more planning than a presentation in a standard conference room.

Different Types of Audiences

Every audience is unique—but types of audiences have specific, common needs. Knowing the "make-up" of your audience is key to successfully communicating with them. Below are several types of audiences that speakers typically encounter and tips on how to effectively interact with them.

The executives

When making a presentation to your direct superiors or other executive managers, make sure the tone and manner in which you present reflects a "suggestive" tone. This type of presentation is more formal than others. As a subordinate, you want to make sure you don't come off as lecturing to your audience or presenting yourself as "one of them". Instead, make a series of suggestions or recommended course of "actions" to your audience. Also, just in case there are questions, always have the facts and figures to back up your recommendations.

The peer group

The key to successfully communicating to this audience is setting a tone of mutual respect and sharing. When presenting to your peers, it is important that you draw them into the presentation by asking them for their opinions, experiences and feedback.

The team

The key to presenting to your own team is using the word "we". If you are part of a group, it is important to acknowledge group success as well as accept group blame.

Special interest groups

The key to communicating with this audience is relating your topic to the "issue" of the special interest group. By showing the audience you understand their issue, you can make an emotional connection with them. Once you have established such a connection, the audience is ready to truly listen to you. Consider the following example:

A corporate executive from a large health care provider was going to make a luncheon presentation to a women's health group. To gain the interest of her audience, the executive focused on how her organisation developed a free health clinic for inner city women. In doing so, she related her presentation message to an issue that was important to her audience.

Mixed groups

When you have a combination of groups, it is important to structure your presentation so that within the first minutes of presenting, you are able to reach out and connect with each subgroup. Depending on the make-up of your audience, you may want to focus your presentation on the main subgroup within your audience. Just make sure you also plan ways to involve the other audience subgroups.

Making Eye Contact with Your Audience

People speak with their eyes as well as their words. One of the best ways to make your audience feel a part of the presentation is through effective eye contact. By making eye contact with members in your audience, you will get their undivided attention and keep them interested in your presentation.

A standard rule of thumb is to make eye contact with an audience member for 3 to 5 seconds or for the duration of a phrase or thought. Be careful not to hold eye contact too long or the audience member may feel intimidated by your stare. In addition, be careful not to have roller coaster eyes-darting glances to audience members all around the room. That is not considered eye contact.

If possible, try combining eye contact with names. If you use nametags or place cards, occasionally incorporate audience members' names when speaking to them. Addressing people directly and making strong eye contact with them will keep an audience involved and interested in your presentation.

Avoiding Common Pitfalls

Don't get caught up in the common mistakes of most presenters. By being aware of the following pitfalls, you can successfully navigate your way to a winning presentation.

Avoid Overdosing on Experts

Many speakers quote so many experts and resources they lose credibility. It's important to be aware of expert knowledge and even to include it where relevant in your presentation. But the presentation IS your presentation.

Communicating with Your Audience

Anyone can speak to an audience. You get up to say what you have to say and sit down. The real question is, "Did your audience get it?" Great presenters don't speak to their audiences; they communicate with them. They consider a presentation a dialogue—and the audience is important.

Maintain Control

If you cannot control your audience, you cannot control your presentation. Given the right circumstances, you may lose control of the audience if questions get out of hand. The best way to handle this situation is to answer succinctly when a question is asked—then move on. Use your agenda to refocus the audience to the task at hand and redirect other questions for a time later in the presentation. Remember you are the speaker and you need to be in control of your audience.

Say "I don't know" but . . .

Those words are OK to say. When you don't know a specific answer, don't bluff. If you are wrong you will lose credibility with your audience. The best way to handle this situation is to say you will find out and get back to them. At the next break, make a few calls to see if you can find out the answer. If you get an answer, provide that information to the group after the break. If not, be sure to follow up with the audience member after the presentation. Either way you will maintain your credibility.

Resist the Urge to Overload

Don't overload your audience with information. When you develop the content of your presentation it is important to remember that your audience needs enough information to make an informed decision, but not every piece of information you have researched for the last ten years. Your presentation should be clear, concise and to the point! Keep it simple!

Bad Delivery Habits

So you write a great presentation and design state-of-the-art visual aids. Then, you stand up in front of the audience and lose them in ten minutes just because of annoying habits. Worst of all, you don't even know what you are doing that is so distracting. Below are some common delivery pitfalls and how to avoid them.

Fillers: "ah", "um", and "and"

These words are fillers. They distract from a presentation's content and diminish authority as a speaker. They also make you seem unprepared. In general, they are used when a pause is needed. Try replacing filler words with nothing-—just a natural silence.

Annoying movements

— Playing with jewelry
— Licking and/or biting your lips
— Constantly adjusting your glasses
— Popping the top of a pen
— Playing with facial hair (men)
— Playing with/twirling your hair (women)
— Jingling change in your pocket
— Leaning against anything for support

Again, these actions can be replaced with something meaningful. If you find yourself nervous—and clicking the top of your pen, move to another location, if possible. Take the sting out of the nervousness by walking towards the audience.

Too many gestures

The only thing worse than using no gestures are using too many gestures. This is not a problem for many people—but if it is for you, try maintaining good eye contact with audience members. It is very difficult to gesture wildly while looking at someone.

Screaming clothing

Loud clothes speak volumes. Unfortunately, they speak over you. Whatever your personal style, tone down your dress a notch or two for your next presentation. Try solid colors—understated jewelry.

Sloppy editing

Misspelled words signify sloppiness and cost credibility. Print out any visual aid and hard edit it. It is much easier to find minor errors in print form.

Turning your back

Don't talk to the projector screen, whiteboard, or flipchart. If you need to refer to a visual, do so with a 45-degree angle.

INTEGRATING MOVEMENT IN PRESENTATIONS

Movement is the key to breaking down the psychological space barriers that exist between the speaker and the audience. As a presenter, you notice this automatic barrier when you give a presentation. You are the speaker—they are the audience, and the audience is on the other side of an imaginary line. In order to break down this artificial barrier, it is imperative that you "cross the line". The easiest and most effective way to do this is through movement.

A speaker should establish three positions in the room to which he/she travels throughout the presentation. The first of these positions is the home position. This position is where you spend most of your time during the presentation. In order to maximise your interaction with the audience, you should refrain from using the podium as this position.

The second position is designed to create a change of pace and increase interest in your presentation.

The second position can be used as a staging area to review visuals such as flipcharts, transparencies or electronic slides. This position is usually directly across from the home position, on the same side of the room. This juxtaposition creates a sense of balance.

The third position is designed for special points in your presentation, and it should be used sparingly. This position is the only one that crosses the imaginary line between you and the audience. When you enter this space, you bridge the gap between you and your audience.

Movement is not complicated to incorporate into a presentation: it simply requires planning. Before your next presentation, arrive early and establish your three positions. Practice when and how you will use these positions. Soon you will learn how to effectively use movement in your presentation.

EASY STEPS TO A GREAT PRESENTATION

Developing a presentation can be a daunting task. What do you do first? Write down notes, choose a slide template, look for research? Maybe a bit of everything? In general, there are four steps to creating a great presentation and they aren't what many people first consider. In fact, most people delve right into choosing artwork or thinking about the organisation without considering the important background questions first.

Step 1 - Background

Before you begin to develop the content of your presentation, you need to know the basics: who you are presenting to, what is the specific topic to cover, what is the format of the presentation, etc.

Step 2 - Content

Once you have finalised the background information, it's time to develop the "meat" of your presentation. This can be the most important task.

Step 3 - Visuals

You also need to create effective visual aids that emphasize key content points. Consult The Numbers on Why You Need Visuals if you want to understand the impact of visual aids. Then, go to the Presenter's Online Resources to download a great PowerPoint template or to find some new clip art.

Step 4 - Delivery

Once you have created your presentation, it's time to practice your delivery skills. Be sure to check out: Making Eye Contact with Your Audience, Integrating Movement in Presentations, 6 Tips for Keeping Your Presentation Interesting for quick tips on improving your delivery technique.

Step 5 - Final Presentation

You have finished your presentation, practiced your delivery, and packed up your visual aids. You think you are set to go. But, do you remember how to set up the projector and connect your laptop? Have you saved a backup copy of your presentation on disk? Don't let technical difficulties kill an otherwise successful presentation.

GETTING YOUR NERVES UNDER CONTROL BEFORE A PRESENTATION

It is no secret that many people do not like to get up in front of an audience to give a presentation. The simple fear of presenting often creates a great amount of nervous energy for a speaker. If this situation strikes you, what can you do with this nervous energy?

The best presenters learn how to take their nervous energy and transform it into presentation presence! By practicing the exercise tips below, you to can turn your fear into a presentation strength. Go for it!

Breathe - Relax - Breathe

Take some deep breaths. Let the air out slowly. Repeat.

Stretch your muscles. Start with your neck, legs and arms.

Repeat the breathing exercises.

Finally, take a moment and close your eyes. Focus on being totally relaxed and prepared. Open your eyes and you should be ready to go!

The Walk

Take a few minutes and stroll through the presentation room before your audience arrives. Visualise yourself giving a successful presentation in various spots in the room. The goal is to make the room feel as if it were your space for success!

Greetings

Take the fear out of the "audience" by greeting them as they enter the room. Say "hello", shake their hands, and start building "friendship" bridges. This simple action can take the mystery out of an audience and help you gain immediate impact as a presenter.

GIVING YOUR FIRST PUBLIC PRESENTATION

Your boss just told you that you will be speaking next week at a luncheon meeting of the local professional marketing association. She said your topic should relate to the award-winning marketing campaign you just completed, but she didn't elaborate on details. You are excited but very nervous. You have never given a presentation before a large group and you don't know where to start. Have no fear! The following checklist should help you get the background information you need to develop an effective presentation.

General Information

Who will be attending?

How does your topic relate to the attendees?

Does this group understand the technical/industry language you may use in your presentation?

How long do you need to speak?

What is the preferred style to present?

Will there be Q&A?

What is the name of the sponsoring organisation and key contact information?

Audience Information

What is the audience size?

What are the basic demographics of the audience (age, gender, race, religion, education level, socio-economic level, etc.)?

What are some of the related interests of the audience?

What will the audience be wearing (audience attire)?

What will be the disposition of the audience (friendly, supportive, neutral, hostile)?

What is the knowledge level of the audience regarding your presentation topic?

Once you have the basic information about your audience, you need to get more information about the logistics of your presentation. This information is critical. You don't want to get caught preparing an hour-long presentation to later find you were to appear on an expert panel for Q&A.

Keeping Your Audience Awake During a Video

Videos are a great way to add visual pizzazz to presentations. However, videos can backfire on you if they put your audience to sleep. Below are some easy tips on how to hold an audience's attention during a video.

Give a preview

Before you show the video, tell your audience what the video is about, what to look for, and what questions you will discuss when it is over. Setting expectations for an audience helps to keep them tuned in while they watch.

Break before the video

Take a break before showing the video. Your audience will be more refreshed and ready to actively view the video when they come back. Be careful though—sometimes people perceive a video as "optional". If you let an audience know you will use the information in the video later in the presentation, they will be sure to watch it.

Listen for the last line

Tell your audience that the most important part of the video is the very last line (if it is in any way true). When you offer this information, your audience will pay close attention to the whole video in an effort to absorb "why" the conclusion is the most important part.

Overcoming Your Fear of Presenting

One of the best ways is to use a self-evaluation exercise to break down your fear into manageable components.

Top Ten Fears

- Speaking before a group
- Heights
- Insects and Bugs
- Financial Problems
- Deep Water
- Sickness
- Death
- Flying
- Loneliness
- Dogs

Self-Evaluation Exercise

Tell yourself exactly what you are afraid of.

— I am afraid of speaking in front of a large group.

Explain to yourself why you are afraid.

— I am afraid because I think everyone will laugh at me. I am afraid something will go wrong.

Tell yourself why you shouldn't be afraid.

— I have never seen a speaker get laughed off the stage. No one has ever laughed at me during a presentation. If something does go wrong, I can fix it.

Close with positive thoughts about yourself.

— I am a smart and out-going person. I can give a solid presentation and impress my audience.

Planning Breaks During Presentations

Effectively planning breaks throughout a presentation keeps an audience alert and interested. As a general rule, you should take a 10-minute break for every hour you speak. Audiences get restless if you do not allow them to stretch, go to the restroom, return a page, etc. In addition, it is difficult for audience members to intently focus on your presentation for an extended period of time. By planning systematic breaks, you enable your audience to focus their attention on you.

Below are some planning tips for breaks.

Plan breaks at strategic points

While it is important to take a break every hour or so, don't stop midway through a key presentation point to take a break. Make sure you finish a point or topic and then take a break.

Set a return time

Don't tell your audience how long a break is. Instead, give them a specific time to return. This avoids any speculation.

Vary the lengths of breaks

Consider, for example, offering a 5-minute break after the first hour of a lengthy presentation. This allows your audience to get a drink of water and run to the restroom. Because the presentation has just begun, their "needs" should be minimal. Give them 15 minutes for the second break. This allows the audience to take care of more time-consuming items. When you allow your audience time to take care of their "outside" items, they can be more attentive and focused when they return.

Ask for their input

If you are unsure of your audience's needs, ask them how much time they need. In coming to a consensus about the break, you establish psychological agreement with them to return on time. It really does work!

PUTTING YOUR BEST IMAGE FORWARD

It is extremely important as a presenter to project a positive image. Audiences evaluate not only what is presented, but who presents it. They may think the information you present is great, but if they are unsure of who is delivering it, you still may not convince your audience to do what you want them to do. Remember the messenger is just as important as the message.

Research shows you have seven seconds before your audience starts forming an opinion about you. That's not a lot of time to put your best foot forward. The key factors in a speaker's image include dress, attitude, tone and knowledge. Fine tuning these factors can help you develop a powerful image.

Dress

— Your dress should communicate a professional image.

— Dress should be conservative unless you know otherwise.

— Men should typically wear a suit.

— Women should wear a suit or skirt and jacket.

— Clothes should be clean and neatly pressed.

— Shoes should be shined.

— You should evaluate the level of dress of your audience and dress one level up.

— Power colors include navy blue, dark gray, and most jewel tones.

Extra tips for women:

— Pearls add credibility.

— Dangling jewelry is distracting.

Attitude

The only attitude that is appropriate for a presentation is an upbeat positive one! No audience wants to listen to an unenthusiastic, disinterested speaker. If you don't have a positive attitude about what you are talking about, why should your audience? There may be on occasion when a speaker should have something other than an upbeat attitude, but this is the exception and not the rule.

Tone

When speaking with your audience, your tone should be confident but not authoritative. The trick is to speak to your audience in a way in which you convey yourself as knowledgeable and confident, but not authoritative or overbearing.

Be sure you speak slowly enough for the audience to follow you. People are frustrated by fast speakers and tend to view those speakers as nervous. When covering the important points, slow down. Audiences will focus in on those specific points, and such concentration will help them retain information after the presentation is over.

Knowledge

Make sure you know what you are talking about! There is nothing more frightening than giving a presentation about something you don't know about. Make yourself take the time necessary to research anything you don't know.

RULES FOR TEAM PRESENTATIONS

The necessity for teamwork in the workplace is not a new idea. However, it is becoming commonplace to find that cooperative effort is needed in all areas of corporate communication. Presentations are no exception. When you work in a group, there are always varying degrees of "teamwork" issues that need to be addressed. Whether it's developing a consistent presentation style and tone, scheduling team meetings or determining who will present.

Team presentations can be a nightmare if you don't get off to a good start. Here are guidelines designed to make your team presentation experience less hectic.

1. Select a Strong Team Leader

This individual should have the leadership ability and authority to make on-the-spot decisions. Whether it's content, structure, presenters, etc, this person needs to take full responsibility for the overall outcome of the presentation.

2. Follow the Same Rules You use when Developing a Solo Presentation

Make sure everyone understands the overall presentation objectives as well as their roles in the development of the final presentation.

3. Organise Content Development

Trying to collectively "write" a presentation is a difficult task. Try arming each person with a stack of Post-it notes. Then, have individuals write only their own ideas (one per note). When it comes time to "write" the presentation, go to a room with a large blank wall and use this flat surface as a clean slate. Organise presentation content on the wall; move topics as desired. Once the content is organised, the group can determine what types of visual aids are needed and where to place them.

4. Keep Visuals with One Person

Be sure one person is assigned to manage the visual aids. By assigning one team member to this task, you can ensure consistent color, style, and format.

5. Provide Transitions

If you have multiple presenters, you need to plan clean transitions between presenters. Smooth, transitions ensure that you convey a well-prepared, professional image.

6. Rehearse, Rehearse, Rehearse

When pulling together a team presentation, it is important that everyone become familiar with presentation content, visual aids, and transitions between presenters. Because everyone presents in a unique way, it is critical that the team practice together in order to reach a high level of comfort with the presentation and each other. A full dress rehearsal with visual aids is a must for a successful team presentation!

TIPS FOR KEEPING YOUR PRESENTATION INTERESTING

Visuals. Visuals. Visuals

Your audience wants you to show them what you are talking about—literally. Use color graphics, slides, and handouts to get your message across. Research shows that your audience will remember more when you use visual aids to reinforce your words.

Ditch the Podium

Don't get stuck using the podium as a security blanket. Get out in front of your audience and interact with them. You don't have to zoom around the room, but make sure you occasionally move around especially when the audience is large.

Use Eye Contact

You are the presenter and the attention is on you. Make sure you maintain eye contact with your audience. As a general rule, you should make eye contact with an audience member for three to five seconds. Also you should try to make eye contact with all areas of the room, including the back of the room.

Focus on Your Audience

Visuals are designed to provide your audience with reinforcement of your verbal points. They are not supposed to be a presentation crutch.

Be Who You are

Don't try and be something you are not. Audiences can smell a fake in a minute. Develop your own presentation style and use it!

Skip the Speech

The worst speakers are those who read straight off their notes. Use notes as reminders, but try not to read them. It is far better to speak naturally and use notes to keep yourself on target.

SIZE OF THE PRESENTATION

A presentation is a presentation right? It doesn't matter whether you are speaking to 5 or 500 people . . . As long as you have a good presentation it will work accordingly. One of the worst commonly overlooked details of giving a presentation is the size of the audience. It is true that the content of the presentation doesn't have to change because of the size of the audience, but the way it's communicated should be quite different!

Small Group (Client Presentation, Work Groups)

When delivering to a group of this size, all of your efforts should be focused on the individuals in your audience. Presentation style, pace, visuals, and group interaction are dictated by your audience. Given the size of this intimate group, it is imperative the audience feels important.

Interactive Group (Training Class, Department Meetings)

An interactive group demands different things than a small group does. For one, the level of involvement with the audience diminishes. While audience interaction is important, a high level of audience interaction is not possible. Instead, the content of the presentation is most important. Visuals should be clear, concise, and help move your audience to better understand the content objectives.

Structured Group (Sales Presentation, Shareholder Meetings)

The key to a presentation of this group size is effectively communicating your message as a speaker with your delivery and visuals. Because this type of presentation is very targeted and the audience knows this, visuals should be specific to the main messages in the presentation.

Big Room Groups (Keynote Speakers, Luncheon Meetings)

If you are speaking to a large audience, you must realise that people are there to see you speak. While the content of your presentation is important, you are part of the reason why they are there. Consequently, it is extremely important that your delivery by dynamic, simple-to-follow, and credible. Your visuals should also be simple so that any audience member is able to see and understand anything that is projected.

Tips for Using Your Voice Effectively

Make sure you speak loud enough for the audience to hear you.

Nothing is worse than having to strain to hear a speaker present. So, before you begin a presentation, have someone stand at the back of the room and tell you if you can be heard.

Don't speak in a monotone voice. The easiest way to put an audience to sleep is by speaking in the same voice for a long period of time. Make sure you use natural speech patterns—with highs and lows—instead of a flat monotone.

Alternate the pace of your voice. By speaking at different speech rates for short periods, you can add energy to your speech pattern. Just look at the way you speak in normal conversation. You will notice that sometimes you speak quickly and sometimes you slow down.

Slow down for important points. By slowing your speech rate for key points, you can emphasize important points.

Use the pause. Silence is an excellent exclamation point. By slightly extending a pause, you can add emphasis to a key point in your presentation. All presenters pause naturally, but the best presenters plan their pauses for maximum impact!

Drink water. Before presenting, have a glass of water. Water can prevent potential voice problems during a presentation. You can also use a sip of water as a pause in a presentation.

The Truth About Laser Pointers

Many presenters like to use laser pointers during their multimedia presentations. In fact, these can be quite useful devices when they perform well. But how reliable are laser pointers?

Have you ever seen a presentation in which the presenter couldn't keep the pointer steady? Your eyes move up and down and you can't concentrate on what the speaker is saying. Or perhaps you have been the presenter? Ever try to juggle the laser pointer, the projector remote and the cordless microphone? All these accessories have value, but they can also hinder smooth transitions and a polished appearance.

The good news is that there is an easier way to highlight want you want without using a laser pointer. Today many multimedia projector manufacturers such as Epson offer "special effects" button on their projector remotes. These buttons allow you to highlight, circle, point, and even zoom on the information you want to highlight. Better yet, you can select the "special effects" that you want and where to place them on your remote.

Delivery" border=0 height=40 src="/images/title_basics_delivery.gif" width=400

TOP TEN MISTAKES MADE BY PRESENTERS

No presentation objectives: If you don't know what your audience should do at the end of your presentation, there is no need for you to present. Knowing your objectives is the key to developing an effective presentation.

Poor visual aids: Visual aids are designed to reinforce the main points of your presentation. Without effective visuals, you are missing a key opportunity to communicate with your audience.

Ineffective close: Closing your presentation is extremely important. The close allows you to tie up the presentation and spell out what you want your audience "to do". A weak close can kill a presentation.

Mediocre first impression: Audiences evaluate a presenter within the first 120 seconds of the presentation. Presenters who make a bad first impression can lose credibility and diminish their ability to effectively communicate.

No preparation: The best presenters prepare for every presentation. Those who prepare and practice are more successful in presenting their information and anticipating audience reaction. Practice does make perfect!

Lack of enthusiasm: If you aren't excited about the presentation, why should your audience be? Enthusiastic presenters are the most effective ones around!

Weak eye contact: As a presenter, you are trying to communicate effectively with your audience. If you don't make eye contact with the audience, they will not take you or your message seriously.

No audience involvement: The easiest way to turn off an audience is by allowing them to remain uninvolved. Use audience involvement to gain "buy-in".

Lack of facial expressions: Effective speakers use facial expressions to help reinforce their messages.

Sticky floor syndrome: There is nothing worse than a speaker who is glued to the floor. While there is no need to wander about aimlessly, natural movement helps hold an audience's attention.

USING A PRESENTATION ASSISTANT

Just when you think you are done . . . you have finished writing your presentation, you have created fabulous slides and handouts, you have analysed room conditions and more . . . What could possibly be left to do? In some cases, it may be time to ask yourself if your presentation would be helped by a "presentation assistant". The more complicated a presentation, the more likely a presentation may prove helpful.

When we speak about an assistant, we speak of someone who can provide an extra set of hands, who knows how to juggle the balls you don't have time to . .

. A presentation assistant can pass out handouts, advance slides, or assist with group exercises.

Tips for Using a Presentation Assistant

— Select an assistant with whom you can work: someone you know and trust.

— Select an assistant who is familiar with your presentation or who can get that way. Set up a meeting and walk through your entire presentation, several times. Identify points at which the assistant should go to the next slide, turn up lights, or pass out appropriate handouts.

— Work out unobtrusive signals for communication.

— And most importantly, when you deliver the presentation, make sure to introduce your assistant.

DON'T GO BLANK DURING YOUR PRESENTATION

You have your audience following intently along. You are going like gangbusters, but then all of a sudden you lose your train of thought. You can't quite remember where you are or where you are going . . . O.K., now you are beginning to panic . . . The first thing to remember is that this situation happens to everyone at some point in time! The key to solving this problem is knowing how to recover, without losing a beat. Here are some sure-fire ways to get your presentation back on track.

1. Don't Freak Out

First and foremost, relax. Don't go into a panic. Audiences can sense panic, and, like sharks, they look for it. Take a deep breath and relax!

2. Always Have Notes

Speakers should always have their speaker notes within reach. After you take a breath and relax, glance at your notes for an idea or trigger to get you back on track. Don't rapidly flip through them like you are searching for the winning lotto numbers; just glance over them in a way that will refresh your memory!

Once you have what you need, pick up where you left off. Audiences don't mind when you refer to your notes. The trick to using notes well is to make it look deliberate. Don't try to get a frantic glimpse of them. Just look at them when necessary and then put them aside.

3. Have "Lifeboat" Questions

The other way to buy some time is to have back-up "lifeboat" questions. These questions should relate to your topic and be broad enough to take some time for your audience to answer, yet not so specific they need to review your presentation. While the audience is working on answering your question, you will have time to get back into the groove of your presentation.

ELIMINATING FILLER WORDS AND ACTIONS

Have you ever attended a presentation—one in which you knew the presenter—and have been astounded by how a seemingly articulate person disappears under pressure? All of a sudden, the colleague who speaks clearly and is respected by his team members stammers and stutters. He interjects "um" and "uh" in every other sentence. Why does this happen?

In general, when speakers say these filler words or do other filler actions (such as licking their lips), they do so unconsciously. They make these sounds or do these actions at a transition point—when they are getting ready to move on to another topic or offer an example. The simple act of switching from one topic to another demands a transition, and when one is not determined, the unconscious fills in. So, for some, it is a less-than-articulate "uh", and for others it is scratching the head. In either case, the behavior can be stopped.

The best way to eliminate filler words and actions is to substitute one behavior for another. So at points of transition, or whenever you feel the need to inject filler, simply pause. Take a deep breath and gather your thoughts. The pause that seems so long to you, pulse-racing, head-pounding, is actually a welcome respite for your audience. They, too need a filler in order to concentrate.

USING MULTIMEDIA PROJECTOR REMOTE CONTROLS

Today many multimedia projector companies have developed projector remotes that allow you to integrate all of your audiovisual controls into one remote control. Whether it's running a corporate video, highlighting a key point in a PowerPoint presentation or turning up the sound volume, you may very well need only one remote control.

WORKING WITH ROOM LAYOUT

Perhaps surprisingly, room layout affects all aspects of a presentation. Just the physical arrangement of chairs can create a feeling of intimacy and cooperation or authority and hierachy. If possible, you should try to select the room layout that works best for you, depending upon audience size, presentation content, and visuals. Below are common room layouts and tips on how and when to use them.

Room Layout Tips

— *Preview the room.* You can avoid most pitfalls with room layout if you visit the venue in advance of your presentation. If possible, speak with the venue staff to make sure that your space is adequate and that they can accommodate all of your presentation needs.

— *Be sure to plan for visuals.* When planning your room layout, make sure you accommodate for your visuals and visual equipment. Leave adequate room to maneuver around all equipment. Test distances for viewing from all angles in the room.

— *Use a Photo.* Take a photo of a room set-up that you like. When you speak with the venue staff, give them the photo to use as a guide when setting up the room.

Theater Style

This layout is primarily used for large audiences. It is also the layout you are least likely to have any control of—chances are, the space is set up for you. Given the size and formality of this layout, it is especially important that you be sure that your audience can see you and your visuals from all areas of the room.

Classroom Style/U-Shaped Style

These layouts tend to be the most effective for educational and training presentations. Classroom style is primarily used for larger audiences, while the U-shaped style is preferred for more intimate training classes. Both of these layouts allow audience members to take notes and participate in group activities. The challenge for the presenter is keeping movement possible—without causing a great deal of disruption. Try to ensure a large adult can walk through any aisle.

Meeting Style

The most popular room layout for small groups is meeting style. The layout allows the presenter to be as formal or informal as he/she wants. In addition, the presenter has a high degree of interaction with the audience. It is important however, that the presenter still be the focus of attention. So, even in an informal setting, the presenter should sit at the "head" of the table or occupy another position of prominence. This is most important when using visual aids.

BIBLIOGRAPHY

Antony Jay, Ros Jay, *Effective Presentation: How to Create and Deliver a Winning Presentation,* Prentice Hall, March 2004.

Bhatia, V. K., *Analysing genre: language use in professional settings,* Harlow, U.K.: Longman, 1993.

Brown, Stephanie Willen, "Indexing Photographs: Presentation at the 1998 Visual Edge Seminar," Special Libraries Association, News Division Web site, http://www.ibiblio.org/slanews/archiving/VE98/presentation.htm

David A. Patterson, *How to Give a Bad Talk,* Computer Science Division, University of California-Berkeley, Circa 1983.

Douglas, S. and Hurst, M., "Layout and language: lists and tables in technical documents", *Punctuation in Computational Linguistics Workshop SIGPARSE 1996,* Santa Cruz, USA. June 1996.

Dubois, Betty Lou, "Poster sessions at biomedical meetings: Design and presentation", *The ESP Journal,* 1985.

Eric Matson, Now That We Have Your Complete Attention, "Here's Fast Company's eight-point program for presentations guaranteed to keep your listeners on the edge of their seats", Illustrations by: Steven Guarnaccia, Feb/Mar 1997.

Feiner, S., "A grid-based approach to automating display layout", *In Proceedings of the Graphics Interface,* pages 192—197, Los Angeles, CA.: Morgan Kaufman, 1988.

Griffith, George W., "Poster sessions: One-to-one technical communication", In Society for Technical Communication (Ed.), *Proceedings: 28th International Technical Communication Conference,* Pittsburgh, PA: Society for Technical Writing, May 20-23, 1981.

Kress, G. and T. V. Leeuwen, *Reading Images: the grammar of visual design*, London and New York, Routledge, 1996.

Larkin, Greg, "Storyboarding: A concrete way to generate effective visuals", *The Journal of Technical Writing and Communication,* 1996.

Lee I., *"Presentation Tips for Public Speaking", A Research Guide for Students.*

Mark D. Hill, *Oral Presentation Advice Computer Sciences,* Department, University of Wisconsin-Madison, April 1992.

Microsoft Office Online, *PowerPoint Tips.*

Reichenberger, K., K. J. Rondhuis, J. Kleinz and J. Bateman, "Effective presentation of information through page layout: a linguistically-based approach", *Proceedings of ACM Workshop on Effective Abstractions in Multimedia, Layout and Interaction,* San Francisco, California, 1995.

Rose, Gillian, *Visual Methodologies: An Introduction to the Interpretation of Visual Materials*, London: Sage Publications, 2001.

Roth, S. F. and Mattis, J., Automating the presentation of information, *In Proceedings of the IEEE Conference on AI Applications,* 90—97. Miami Beach, FL.: IEEE, 1991.

Scherer, Joanna C., "You Can't Believe Your Eyes: Inaccuracies in Photographs of North American Indians," *Studies in the Anthropology of Visual Communication* 2, Fall 1975.

Steven J. Bell, Director, Paul J. Gutman, "Oh No! I Can't Get on the Web: Offline Strategies for Internet Content Presentations", Library, Philadelphia University, Searcher Vol.8, March 2000.

Weinstein-McShane, "Ruth, Collegial sharing through poster sessions", *TESOL Journal,* 1997.

White, J. T., "Technical poster fabrication", In Society for Technical Communication (Ed.), *Proceedings: 28th International Technical Communication Conference,* Pittsburgh, PA; Society for Technical Writing, May 20-23, 1981.

INDEX